DATE			

MIRAMBO OF TANZANIA

1840?-1884

Photograph of Mirambo taken in the 1880s.

MIRAMBO OF TANZANIA
1840?-1884

NORMAN ROBERT BENNETT

NEW YORK
OXFORD UNIVERSITY PRESS
London   1971   Toronto

PREFACE

I BEGAN WORK on Mirambo while studying the history of nine-teenth-century East Africa with the aid of a Foreign Area Train-ing Fellowship from the Ford Foundation. Additional support came in later years from Boston University's African Studies Pro-gram through its directors, William O. Brown and A. A. Castagno. Father John B. Kabeya kindly gave me an English translation of his important Swahili work, *Mtemi Mirambo*. Miss Irene M. Fletcher, archivist of the Congregational Council for World Mis-sion, provided her usual thorough help for those working in the records of the London Missionary Society; she also provided the illustrations of Mirambo and E. J. Southon in this volume, which appear by the kind permission of the Congregational Council for World Mission. Earlier versions of parts of Mirambo's career appeared in my *Studies in East African History* (Boston Univer-sity Press, 1963), and in the periodicals *African Affairs* and *Tan-ganyika Notes and Records*. The directors of these organizations kindly gave their permission for the re-use of the materials in-cluded in these studies. My thanks go to all those named above for their willing help.

My special thanks go to Andrew Roberts of the University of Zambia for helpful comments on the first draft of the manuscript, to Marguerite Ylvisaker, Susanne Marcus, Polly Horn, and Ann McGonigle for their labors in preparing the final copy of the manuscript, and to Ruth Bennett, for sacrificing her own work to aid my completion of Mirambo's biography.

N.R.B.

Marseilles and Boston

September 1969–May 1970

CONTENTS

INTRODUCTION

MIRAMBO, a nineteenth-century leader of the numerous Nyamwezi peoples of central Tanzania, has captured the historical imaginations of contemporary Tanzanians and other East Africans, as well as of many non-Africans, with the universal reputation of being one of the truly great indigenous leaders of that turbulent period of African history just before the European conquest and domination of eastern Africa. Some might object that there was no Tanzania during the years of Mirambo's activities, arguing instead that Mirambo was merely a great leader among the Nyamwezi, and, at that, not even among all the Nyamwezi. But Tanzanian citizens of today operate within the boundaries drawn by their former European rulers, both in politics and in history, and they regard Mirambo as occupying an honored place in their past.

However, there are still some important questions about Mirambo's career which have not been fully answered in the few brief analyses of the Nyamwezi leader. What is Mirambo famous for in the history of East Africa? Was he merely a leader of warriors whose victories led to the creation of a large but short-lived African state? If Mirambo was more than a military commander, just what did he do to impress both his contemporaries and members of later generations? And finally, there remain the most difficult questions of all: what was the rationale in Mirambo's

mind for what he attempted, and what in his personality contributed to the successes and failures he gained? I will attempt to
answer these questions.

Mirambo first drew my attention because of the central position
he occupied in the affairs of the Arabs and Europeans active
during the 1870's and 1880's in the central regions of the future
Tanzania. Since most of the important historical currents of
nineteenth-century East Africa seemed significantly to involve
Mirambo in one way or another, he was a natural figure for additional study. But at this stage in the process of studying nineteenth-century East African history, it is extremely rare for the
historian to possess enough source materials to allow satisfactory
reconstruction of the profile of an African individual. For the
few African leaders for which adequate historical materials are
available, another problem occurs, one common to all non-literate
societies. A main strength of any biography, if we really want to
understand the subject, should be the information, and infer-
ences, gained from the character's own thoughts and words,
whether preserved in his letters, diaries, speeches, or in the memories of individuals who either knew the subject personally or
have preserved oral traditions concerning his career. How else
can we understand the individual process of decision making
except through examining the thought patterns of the individual
concerned?

Very few of the above materials are available to a biographer of
Mirambo. The Nyamwezi leader left no reasoned explanations
to justify the decisions he made at important moments of his
career. What information we do have is from his reported conversations with Europeans and Arabs, from the letters several
Europeans said Mirambo dictated to them, and from a few oral
accounts recorded from the memories of Nyamwezi who either
knew Mirambo or had been told of him by their predecessors. It
is a very uneven record. Nevertheless, Mirambo was so much at
the center of events in the central Tanzania of his era, when
Europeans in significant numbers first began intruding into the
interior regions of East Africa to begin the process which changed
the whole direction of Mirambo's world, that there is a sufficient
body of information about his career to make a biography pos-

sible. Many questions remain unanswered, but as with the historical lacunae in the careers of most other leaders of the African past, they may never be capable of satisfactory solution. At least with Mirambo we can attempt a fairly detailed recounting of many of the events of his busy career.

And it is without question an important career. Mirambo had a part in almost all the major historical trends affecting his region: the rise and decline of the Arab position among the Nyamwezi, the successes and failures of the first European missionaries, the sluggish progress of Leopold II of Belgium and his International African Association, the efforts of the British Consul General in Zanzibar to spread his influence inland. Mirambo influenced these and many other developments emanating from outside his territory. In internal African affairs Mirambo had a similar influence, probably even a more important one. Mirambo dominated events among the Nyamwezi for several decades, and he had a dominating role in the areas of many other contiguous African peoples as he attempted to expand the authority of his state to create, as he did for a time, the largest political entity of his region.

Mirambo was a successful warrior and a peaceful administrator, a skillful diplomat and an intimate friend of missionaries. He rose from being the unimportant leader of a very small African state to become so significant a ruler that his aid was sought, and his views were discussed, in the several centers of Europe then directing their interest to East Africa. Mirambo's life is the story of a talented individual of nineteenth-century East Africa who in responding to the great changes brought by that century to Africa launched a spectacular career. The successes and failures Mirambo faced during this career are the subject of this biography.

MIRAMBO OF TANZANIA

1840?-1884

I

THE NYAMWEZI AND
THE ARABS

NYAMWEZI SOCIETY

THE WESTERN CENTRAL REGIONS of the modern East African state
of Tanzania are dominated by a vast rolling plateau, its surface
broken by frequent ridges and littered with large, tortured
granite outcrops, which stretches on all sides as far as man can
see. It is a high plateau, with elevations ranging from 3000 to
4500 feet, although most of the region is between 3800 and 4200
feet high, thus providing conditions for a temperature that varies
over the course of the year from about 48° to 72° Fahrenheit.
The more elevated land, where most of the population resides
and works, is covered with what is known locally as *miombo* bush
vegetation (scientifically, vegetation characterized by the Brachy-
stegia-Isoberlina association), a designation describing a dry
woodland and forest region. Much of this land is of very little
use for agriculture since its soil is not rich and it lacks ground-
water. The plateau's year has two basic seasons. During the dry
season, from April to October, when often no rain falls at all,
central Tanzania can become a very inhospitable area for man
and beast; even the few rivers which flow through the region
often completely dry up. The season of rains lasts from October
to April, and the average annual rainfall is about thirty-five
inches. The rainfall is uncertain, varying greatly from location
to location and from season to season. Consequently, famines

3

have been, and remain, a frequent threat to the lives of the peoples of the region.

Within this normally harsh environment, which is not an unusual one for most of Tanzania, live the Bantu-speaking peoples known as the Nyamwezi, one of the largest of the 124 tribal groupings of Tanzania. That country's last census with tribal breakdowns (1957) listed them as numbering 363,258. Just to the north of the Nyamwezi live the Sukuma peoples, a closely related group—the word "sukuma" means "north" in the language of the Nyamwezi—who are the largest tribal grouping within Tanzania, comprising in 1957 a total of 1,093,767 individuals. Because of the many similarities in all aspects of their cultures, both the Nyamwezi and the Sukuma groupings are often regarded as forming basically one people; certainly there are no sharp differentiations among the populations of their border regions. Both peoples were markedly affected by Mirambo's career.

During the nineteenth century (and continuing to the present), the Nyamwezi made their living principally through agricultural pursuits, working diligently with iron hand-hoes to cultivate their crops of sorghum, millets, sweet potatoes, beans, maize, and cassava. All members of the population were actively engaged in wresting an adequate livelihood from their uncertain environment all during the season of rains, with the harvest occurring toward September. Once the tasks of the harvest were accomplished, little time was devoted to agriculture until the return of the rains. The raising of cattle also had an important place in Nyamwezi society; the animals, however, had a very irregular territorial distribution owing to the widespread presence of the fatal tsetse fly and to lack of water. Most individual herders, therefore, possessed only limited numbers of cattle. There were wider distributions of other livestock, especially of sheep and goats. The ownership of cattle was important to the course of Nyamwezi life; they were normally the most important items of inheritable property and they were used for bridewealth and to pay customary duties and fines. But cattle did not possess the important ritual worth placed upon them in neighboring cattle-complex areas. Even during the nineteenth century cattle were a valuable marketable commodity, often sold to nearby peoples. The Gogo, for example, bartered ivory, which the Nyamwezi then carried to the markets of the East African coast, for cattle. Interestingly enough, cattle were often separated from the normal way of Nyamwezi life since their entire care was at times left to Tusi immigrants from the interlacustrine areas of Lake Victoria and Lake Tanganyika. These Tusi, forming a sub-culture which had no important bearing upon Nyamwezi life, generally went along with their cattle charges, as several examples from Mirambo's campaigns demonstrate, when Nyamwezi or other raiders seized livestock. A final subsidiary, but important, occupation for the Nyamwezi was hunting; their region was extremely rich in wild life, especially the elephant whose ivory gave the Nyamwezi a prime trading commodity.

Although their cultures were basically the same, neither the Nyamwezi nor the Sukuma had ever been a single politically united group. Far from it, the Nyamwezi were divided into varying numbers of independent chieftainships; the Roman Catholic missionary F. Bösch, the author of one of the earliest extensive studies on the Nyamwezi, gave their number in the nineteenth century as over 150. Following the extensive political changes brought by European rule, Nyamwezi chieftainships numbered 31 during the final years of British administration in Tanzania. The territorial extent and the size of the population of each chieftainship was determined by the geography of its region and by political accident. During the politically fluid times of the nineteenth century the Nyamwezi, in their numerous separate groupings, lived in large, strongly stockaded settlements (called *limbuda*). The populations clustered for safety within the walls around the residences of their chiefs, or in secondary centers, around those of the chiefs' subordinate headmen. In exceptional cases, notably at Mirambo's capital, the number of inhabitants was in the thousands; customarily the numbers were much smaller.

The different chiefly dynasties ruling the separate Nyamwezi political entities each claimed a distinct origin; they related generally similar stories explaining the arrival of their ancestors as hunters in the Nyamwezi regions, probably in the seventeenth

or eighteenth century. The exact historical details of these arrivals, however, still remain unclear. Once established, either on
unoccupied land or in the territories of peoples they subjected
by conquest, persuasion, or other means, the new arrivals founded
minor states. But various problems, probably relating to the size
of the state, which the then limited techniques of political rule
could not solve, led to a continuing fragmentation into the
numerous independent dynasties, which often claimed relationships with each other.

Within this fluid society one key institution, the chiefdom
(the *butemi* or *ichalo*), served as the normal focus of men's activities. At the focal point of the *butemi* was the chief, or *ntemi,*
who in earlier times generally succeeded to office through matrilineal succession. Before the many changes brought about by
the opening of the Nyamwezi world to outside influences during
the nineteenth century, changes which made the career of Mirambo possible, it seems certain that the Nyamwezi *ntemi* was pri-
marily a ritual figure, with, as was common in many states in
all parts of Africa, a vital connection between his person and the
continued successful functioning of his state. Without a healthy
ntemi to represent his people, every aspect of the life of the chiefdom was in serious jeopardy: the rains for successful cultivation
would not fall, the military victories either preserving or extending the state would not be won, the booty from successful campaigns would not be gained. Thus the *ntemi* necessarily played
a central and active role in a comprehensive range of ceremonies
dedicated to bringing success and prosperity to his subjects.

Apart from his participation in these ceremonial functions,
the *ntemi* was required to live a very restricted life, never traveling beyond the established boundaries of his chiefdom, and
always moving about within it under careful guard. The few
direct administrative duties the *ntemi* did perform were confined
to settling disputes among subjects living close to his residence
and, most important of all, to attending annual meetings where
he presided over all his major subordinates. At these gatherings
discussions were conducted concerning the general course of
affairs within the chieftainship and decisions were made about
the policies to be followed during the oncoming year. During

these deliberations the headmen delivered to the *ntemi* that part of the tribute due to him which they had collected from his subjects, plus any other amounts resulting from fines, booty, etc. Before the advent of trade with the distant outside world, this tribute was usually given in livestock and foodstuffs, perishable commodities which the *ntemi* was then expected to share with his subjects in public ceremonies.

Consequently the *ntemi* had practically no role in the actual governing of his people. Even if he had wanted a more active role, the Nyamwezi ruler lacked an independent arm of authority to enforce his wishes. A troublesome headman could be contained only if the other headmen and the *ntemi* acted together either to restrain or to remove the offender. Clearly, then, the important headmen carried out most of the significant duties of administration in the *butemi*, the functions which maintained the political fabric of any single Nyamwezi state. They were the chief administrators and warriors; they controlled the major subdivisions of the greater political entity, each possessing his own regional court to allow him to maintain order and to collect revenues. They maintained their individual lines of descent through patrilineal succession. Most of the headmen appear to have been the descendants of the *ntemis* of their own state, but their ranks did include representatives of former independent dynasties absorbed into a rival state. As a final stark limitation of the *ntemi*'s position, he was strangled if he became seriously ill, a vitally necessary action since all believed that the well-being of the state was identified with his person. During the immediate interregnum, which was kept secret, a new *ntemi* was designated from among the deceased chief's matrilineal descendants through the means of a divination ceremony organized by special ritual officials and by the important headmen, no member of this group being himself eligible for the succession.

The traditional Nyamwezi state thus operated through a union of ritual and administrative functions shared by the *ntemi* and his important headmen, with the actual conduct of the daily operation of the *butemi* being left to the *ntemi*'s theoretical subordinates. His supreme position, although severely limited in practice, was nevertheless secure since his headmen and court

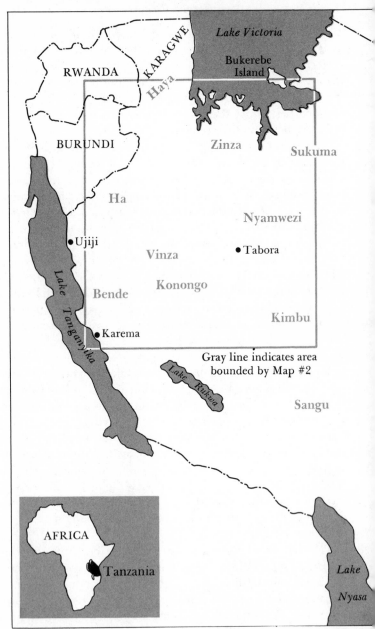

Map 1. TANZANIA. Tribal names appear in light gray.

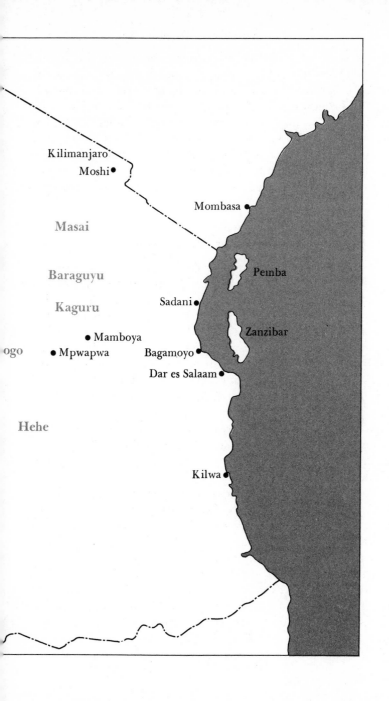

officials were all ineligible to succeed him under the normal laws of succession. This system, functioning as the nineteenth century began, had to face the vastly changed political, economic, and social conditions of life brought about by the opening of the lands of the Nyamwezi to commerce coming from the Indian Ocean littoral. The ensuing modifications among the traditional patterns of Nyamwezi conduct, especially in the role of the *ntemi,* are perhaps best typified by Mirambo and the changes he wrought in the operation of that once secularly powerless office.

THE NYAMWEZI AND COMMERCE

The single most important characteristic of the Nyamwezi, as far as the transformation of their traditional society was concerned, was their propensity for travel far beyond their tribal frontiers. One principal reason for this development must have been the conditions brought about by the recurrent severe famines in Unyamwezi (the land of the Nyamwezi), making it imperative for the Nyamwezi to seek out other ways of gaining successful livelihood. And once the idea of travel had become established in their society, it became a principal course of conduct, whether there was famine or not, since it brought to both the state and to individuals wealth which could never have been secured through agriculture alone. Once gained, the taste for adventure also played its part among this naturally vigorous people.

Thus profiting substantially from their propitious central location on trade routes between many other African peoples, the Nyamwezi early emerged as one of the most active indigenous trading communities of east central Africa. If the rains led to a satisfactory harvest, a Nyamwezi, either in groups organized for strength under the direction of an elected leader, or as an individual, could, for example, travel westward with agricultural produce to nearby Uvinza, there to barter his commodities for salt, an always desired product in inland Africa because of its scarceness. If the harvest was inadequate, the would-be Nyamwezi trader could still travel, even with no commercial commodities,

Map 2. UNYAMWEZI.

instead laboring among the Vinza in their saltworks to earn the salt he could not trade for. With this product, however obtained, the enterprising Nyamwezi could then travel on to trade with more distant peoples, using the condiment to pay for what was needed en route, whether for provisions, water, or passage money (called *hongo* in East Africa), on the march to his destination. Other commodities in demand throughout inland Africa, such as iron hoes, could be gained and distributed in a similar manner.

This peripatetic mode of life brought the Nyamwezi, by about 1800, to regions as far distant as Katanga in Central Africa, from whence they secured and distributed that region's copper widely among eastern African peoples and, even more importantly, as far as to the shores of the Indian Ocean. Furthermore, it was a way of life for the Nyamwezi which would continually develop, taking them into many new regions as the nineteenth century went on. Every enterprising Nyamwezi considered himself bound to set forth on a long and usually dangerous journey to distant markets, especially to those of the very different world of the Arab-influenced coast of East Africa. In the words of the British missionary bishop, Edward Steere, who frequently talked to Nyamwezi arrivals in Zanzibar, any Nyamwezi who did not visit the coast was regarded by his compatriots as a "milksop."[1] Additional comments came from later visitors to Unyamwezi, who reported Nyamwezi youths imitating their elders, and preparing for their future travels, by carrying around mock burdens on their developing shoulders. By the 1880's one observer, the French missionary François Coulbois, estimated that from 15,000 to 20,000 Nyamwezi *pagazi* (carriers) yearly journeyed to the coastal ports.[2] And by the close of the nineteenth century there were colonies of Nyamwezi settlers exercising varying degrees of influence upon the caravan routes in all regions of east central Africa from the eastern Congo to the coast.

But major developments from outside the world of the Nyamwezi were necessary to allow this interior commercial network, the result of so much Nyamwezi pioneering endeavor, to evolve

[1] Edward Steere, "On East African Tribes and Languages," *The Journal of the Anthropological Institute of Great Britain and Ireland*, I (1871), cl.

[2] François Coulbois, *Dix Années au Tanganyka* (Limoges, 1901), 41.

into a primary factor for reshaping life in Unyamwezi and the rest of east central Africa. The African interior had all too few commodities which were of any special interest to the operators of the markets of Asia, Europe, and America. And the few commodities east central Africa did produce, such as ivory and copper, apart from slaves, suffered from the crippling disadvantage of one of the world's most inefficient systems of transport. There were no broad, straight highways of travel into the interior of east central Africa, since the widespread presence of the tsetse fly, accompanied by the serious seasonal water shortages, made animal transport, and the use of wheeled vehicles, impossible. Moreover, north of the Zambesi River there were no rivers of any size navigable enough for significant use in long-distance trade. All commodities had perforce to be carried on the shoulders and heads of men, along narrow and winding paths, which during the season of rains became treacherous quagmires. One British missionary in 1878 thus described the plight of his caravan: "The pagasi train was now a row of black heads on the surface of the water each surmounted by a load."[3] This method of transport, because of its high cost per unit of weight carried, effectively prevented almost all regional products from successfully competing in world markets. And even with the one commodity which could withstand such detrimental conditions and still remain competitive, ivory, there was little hope for extensive commercial success at the beginning of the nineteenth century. The East African coast then possessed no port well enough developed to handle the complex requirements of the world-market economy.

THE EAST AFRICAN COAST

The commercial developments which had already occurred along the East African littoral by the early years of the nineteenth century cannot, of course, be forgotten. Beginning with the small ports facing the barren Somali hinterland, and continuing southward past the many minor centers on the coasts of present-day

[3] Hore to Mullens, Feb. 18, 1878, Journals: Central Africa, 1878-1880, Congregational Council of World Missions Archives, London [hereafter CCWM].

Kenya and Tanzania to the neglected outposts of the Portuguese colonial empire in Mozambique, there already existed an ancient maritime economy. Arab, Persian, Indian, and other enterprising merchants had for millennia utilized the regular monsoon winds of the Indian Ocean, blowing from the northeast from about October to February, and from the southwest for the remainder of the year, to trade for the limited products available along the length of the East African coast. At various times gold, slaves, and ivory were among the favored products. This pattern continued through the centuries, with most of its details—what few remain —still left to be uncovered by the skills of the archaeologist, until the epochal changes brought forth by the career of the Arabian prophet, Muhammad. Then the revitalized Islamic inhabitants of Arabia and the Persian Gulf regions began a process of inter- action with African peoples that is still continuing over broad areas of the African continent.

The continued visits of these Muslim traders, who naturally followed the patterns established by their ancestors, led to in- creased settlement and intermarriage, creating an Afro-Asiatic community, which followed the tenets of Islam, along the stretch of the East African coast. The community became a permanent, albeit a secondary, fringe area of the greater Islamic Indian Ocean world, prospering or stagnating according to the fluctua- tions of the commercial life of the ocean's main centers. This Afro-Asiatic amalgam developed a series of small but prosperous city-states extending along the entire coast, including such centers as Manda, Pate, Mogadoxio, Mombasa, Kilwa Kisiwani, Malindi, and Zanzibar. Until the disruptive arrival of the Portuguese in- vaders at the end of the fifteenth century no one political power, based either in or outside of East Africa, had managed to domi- nate this entire coast. The city-states nevertheless had maintained commercial prosperity without political unity. The Portuguese conquerors, able by their superior military skills to defeat all Indian Ocean rivals and thereby maintain themselves as the dominant force north of Mozambique until about 1700, did achieve a form of political control. But their monopolistic com- mercial practices, joined to their conception of the Portuguese role as crusader against Islam, largely brought about an end to the prosperity that was gained when the city-states were independent.

Omani invaders from southeastern Arabia, summoned by the coastal inhabitants to aid in the overthrow of their Christian rulers in the late seventeenth century, successfully ended the Portuguese presence north of Mozambique, but they were not able to bring a continued state of peace and prosperity to the region. The indigenous populations, with their Portuguese oppressors gone, soon seized every opportunity to regain the independence they all desired, a process facilitated periodically when unsettled political conditions in their Arabian homeland made them indifferent to the East African dominions. Nevertheless, all during the eighteenth century, the coastal ports and their citizens were really more an integral part of the Indian Ocean world than of the African continent. It was not until around 1800 that a vital interaction began between the coastal inhabitant and the African of the interior, and as far as the central regions of present-day Tanzania were concerned, the individuals making this interaction possible were the Nyamwezi.

Two separate developments helped to accomplish this momentous joining of the separate African worlds of the central plateau and the coast. First, as the coastal regions increasingly fell under the sway of the Omani Arabs, the rise of a flourishing plantation economy in the French colonial possessions of Ile de France and Bourbon (now called Mauritius and Réunion), two islands located to the east of Madagascar, resulted in the establishment of a continuing and increasing demand for African workers. No men had inhabited these two isolated islands before the European incursion into the Indian Ocean, but the inherent agricultural and commercial possibilities had been realized through the work of dedicated men like Bertrand-François Mahé de la Bourdonnais and Pierre Poivre. Ile de France and Bourbon developed into important calling stations for French Indian Ocean trading vessels and as centers for the profitable exploitation of valuable agricultural commodities, especially spices and coffee. Thus the importation of slaves became vital to the islands' prosperity, and since the relatively nearby island of Madagascar proved unsatisfactory to meet this need, French traders soon began to seek out East African ports in the effort to meet their slave requirements. With them, a trade which had not been of major importance to East Africa before this time now began its increasingly harmful development. When the European demand ended during the nineteenth century because of British and French efforts to end the sea-borne slave trade, the long-standing trade in slaves to Arabia, the Persian Gulf, and neighboring regions—of which we know few details—continued. The search for slaves in East Africa therefore persisted throughout most of the nineteenth century. The result, disregarding the incalculable suffering involved, brought commercial prosperity to some East African ports, especially in the southern region around Kilwa, while the search for new sources of slaves sent Arab and African traders ever farther into the African interior.

SAID BIN SULTAN AND THE RISE OF ZANZIBAR

The second change of importance in the process of bringing the East African coast and interior into permanent contact came about largely through the efforts of one man. Said bin Sultan, after several troubled years of dynastic intrigue, secured power as the accepted—as much as that term could apply to his disorderly state—ruler of Oman in 1806. By about 1815 this new ruler of the Busaidi dynasty managed to triumph over all of his enemies, domestic and foreign, thus to preside securely over his state, a state divided between the commercially sophisticated inhabitants of Muscat, the capital and a port city that was an important center of the Indian Ocean trading community, and the tribes of the religiously narrow-minded hinterland, who were little concerned with the non-Muslim world. Said bin Sultan's sympathies always lay with the former group. "I am above all a merchant, he liked to say of himself," reported a French visitor to Muscat in the 1850's.[4]

Once his rule appeared secure, the vigorous young sovereign began to pay increasingly more attention to the loose and imperfect dominion which his predecessors had established over the

4 A. De Gobineau, *Trois Ans en Asie* (Paris, 1859), 99.

...s subjects should support his experiment; local tradi-
...that he ordered them to plant three clove trees for
...onut palm that they owned. Conditions for growth
...eal and both islands soon were on a path of develop-
...ich made them the world's largest producers of cloves.
...for example, Zanzibar exported 4,860,000 pounds of
...y the mid-twentieth century Zanzibar and Pemba were
...ng over 80 per cent of the world harvest of the crop, with
...age annual production of about 11,000 tons. The success
...important experiment had significant consequences for
...rican mainland. Cloves are harvested twice yearly, the
...on requiring a large labor force since the marketable spice
...product of the buds of the tree, which have to be picked
...a relatively short period. Zanzibar's indigenous African
...itants, whose land was progressively taken for the growth
...clove trees, were not numerous enough to handle the crop,
...if they had proved willing, and therefore from this time
...rd a continuously increasing number of slaves from the
...land was necessary to secure a successful harvest.
...lied to the creation of a desirable export crop for Zanzibar
...e Said bin Sultan's next steps designed to draw other foreign
...ders, in addition to the Indians, to his African entrepôt.
...ropean traders had visited Zanzibar from before the first years
...Said bin Sultan's reign, particularly in search of slaves, but
...eir numbers had gradually dwindled during the early nine-
...enth century, notably after the Moresby Treaty of 1822, which
...e Arab ruler had signed with Great Britain, forbidding within
...is dominions the selling of slaves to the subjects of Christian
...ations. However, while British, French, and other Europeans
...vere slow to rise to the opportunities offered by the new legiti-
...mate commercial center of Zanzibar, American merchants, particularly from New England, in the search for new outlets for their
maritime enterprise began to investigate the commercial possibilities of the East African ports. Reaching Zanzibar, probably
during the second half of the decade after 1810, the Americans
found the unregulated commercial life of the island port little
to their liking. They emphatically complained about the varying
port charges and customs duties charged by the sultan's officials.

East African coastal city-states. From 1813 Said bin Sultan strove
to bring them firmly under his rule. It was a slow and difficult
task, but by the final defeat in 1839 of his most stubborn coastal
opponents, the Arab Mazrui family, the rulers of Mombasa, Said
bin Sultan once and for all emerged as the single dominant force
upon the East African coast from the Somali regions to the Portuguese holdings in Mozambique. In the course of the often violent
proceedings, especially at the tenacious center of Mombasa, the
Omani ruler had made several visits to East Africa, notably to
the fertile island of Zanzibar. This low-lying island, possessing
one of the most enjoyable tropical climates on earth, had an
adequate harbor and was protected by its twenty-mile distance
from the African mainland against all potentially hostile African
peoples. Said bin Sultan, already as much a merchant prince as
a political ruler, was impressed by the potentialities of Zanzibar
for extensive commercial and agricultural development, as well
as by an environment much more favorable than that provided
by his harsh Arabian homeland. Consequently, in 1840 he, in
effect, permanently transferred the capital of his widespread
dominions to Zanzibar.

While this extremely capable Arabian ruler was consolidating
his dynastic claims to the East African coast, the African populations of the interior, above all the Nyamwezi, were reaching a
stage of political evolution which made permanent contact possible between their home areas and the coast. Long-distance trade,
in East Africa as in other parts of the world, requires stable political entities to provide the safe routes and the secure markets
necessary for conditions of profitable exchange. There are indications that such conditions were beginning to be present by the
1780's. According to Ganda traditions, the African state of
Buganda, which was located to the north of Lake Victoria and
which was already emerging as one of Africa's most centralized
political entities, then began to receive commodities originating
from the East African coast. It is possible that these foreign imports were carried, at least through part of the long distance inland, to Buganda by the Nyamwezi. The details are yet unclear,
but we do know that political development along the trade routes
was then sufficiently under way to allow Nyamwezi traders to

begin moving successfully to the coast. They reached the coastal regions by at least 1800. With this significant breakthrough accomplished, the Nyamwezi only had to take advantage of the commercial and agricultural developments which Said bin Sultan later brought about to become the major trading people operating on the routes leading inland from the several small ports located on the coast opposite Zanzibar.

Said bin Sultan met the opportunity offered by the inland African traders, becoming therefore the real founder of modern East Africa, providing it a geographical and cultural focus and framework which still remains despite the many great changes wrought by the British and German conquerors of the nineteenth and twentieth centuries and their independent African successors. The Arab ruler pursued a series of policies destined to develop the port of Zanzibar, a center described in 1799 by a British officer as possessing only "some few houses, and the rest are huts of straw mat,"[5] as the political, maritime, and commercial hub of the East African world. It was a formidable task; even as late as 1839 an American missionary visitor said slightingly of Zanzibar: "Most of the buildings are mere huts, built of mud and sticks."[6] Said bin Sultan's success can be measured from the fact that European visitors of the later nineteenth century were impressed enough at the result of his handiwork to describe Zanzibar as "the Paris of East Africa."

Said bin Sultan's first important step was to establish Zanzibar as the one significant commercial entrepôt for his entire East African dominions. Thus, once all rivals to Said bin Sultan's predominance were quieted, and the hitherto minor port of Zanzibar became an entirely secure base, the island was ready to attract the first vital segment of the new system, merchants from India. (We will use the nineteenth-century designation of India to cover the area located within the modern states of India and Pakistan.) In limited numbers, such individuals, both Muslim and Hindu, had already become active along the East African

coast; they were virtually the c
ruler with the necessary skills a
his aims. The Indian merchant
wealthy mercantile houses of Bom
most important commercial cente
bin Sultan's Arabian capital of M
had drawn about 2000 Indians the
profitable existence made possible
littoral of East Africa, the Indian n
there in slowly increasing numbers.
sources and commercial experience la
and African subjects of Said bin Sulta
for Zanzibar and for the Nyamwezi, can
cially during and after the 1830's whe
always served as the Customs Master o
dominions. This official held the most imp
bin Sultan's very limited bureaucracy. Th
ceived his office for the payment of an annu
The amount formed practically the enti
Arabian ruler, and, since the sum was insuffi
sive tastes of Said bin Sultan and his succes
into debt to their Indian subordinate. In
Sultan Barghash bin Said owed the firm of th
$540,003. Thus, in many ways, the occupant
virtually the first minister of Zanzibar. Without
ment the sultan lacked the means to muster suf
for any new policies. And, with the Customs M
interest in the development of commerce, the la
played a major role in the organizing of the Ara
resident among the Nyamwezi of the Unyanyembe

Said bin Sultan's second step was to develop a
milieu for the Indians to operate in profitably. One
vance came with his introduction of the cultivation of
Zanzibar and its neighboring island, Pemba, during
around 1820. This spice, originally brought through t
of Pierre Poivre from the Dutch East Indian islands t
France and Bourbon in the eighteenth century, was tr
both in Zanzibar and in Pemba. Said bin Sultan was dete

that all hi
tion says
every coo
proved i
ment wh
In 1859
cloves.
produci
an aver
of this
the Af
operat
is the
within
inhab
of th
even
forw
mai

A
wer
tra
Eu
of
th
te
t
h

---

[5] Quoted in F. B. Pearce, *Zanzibar: The Island Metropolis of Eastern Africa* (New York, 1967), 187.

[6] "Extracts from the Journal of Mr. Hume," *The Missionary Herald*, 36 (1840), 60.

Said bin Sultan was receptive to their protests, arranging with the United States in 1833 Zanzibar's first commercial treaty with a Western power. The treaty, in essentials, established very favorable conditions for American trade, with a 5 per cent import duty being the only tax on merchandise. The United States also received the right to appoint a resident consul; he arrived in 1837 to become the first permanent official representative of a Western nation in Zanzibar. American merchants at once took advantage of these propitious opportunities to dominate trade, apart from Zanzibar's Indian outlets; this lasted until the American Civil War. And once that war was over, the Americans remained among the most important buyers of East African ivory until the trade declined during the early years of the twentieth century. Faced with this competition, and drawn by the profits realized by the Americans, the European merchants interested in East Africa followed the American pattern; treaties similar to that of 1833 were concluded by Great Britain in 1839, France in 1844, and the Hanseatic States in 1859. One measure of Said bin Sultan's success was the 1851 lament of one harassed American merchant who had to face the increasing competition for Zanzibar's wares: "There is entirely too much foreign trade for the place."[7] Said bin Sultan would have been pleased by the complaint.

By this period the trade in slaves was almost entirely restricted to Arabs and Africans, at least on a large scale, so that other products were necessary to retain the foreign resident merchant community drawn from India, the United States, and Europe. Zanzibar and Pemba islands supplied only cloves and the several products of the coconut palm. The nearby African mainland had little to offer apart from gum copal (used in the making of varnish), oil seeds, and hides. All these products could not have sustained Zanzibar at the level of prosperity Said bin Sultan aimed for without the addition of East Africa's most valuable export commodity, ivory. This sought-after product drawn from the African interior had been exported from East Africa since earliest times. It was in demand in all the markets of the world—

---

[7] J. F. Webb to Shepard, Nov. 10, 1851, Shepard Papers, Box 47, Peabody Museum, Salem, Mass.

from the United States to China. The need for ivory during the
nineteenth century was without limit for use in a varied series of
products ranging from carvings to billiard balls and combs. And
with the export of ivory, Zanzibar had a secure base for its
commercial prosperity.

Thus followed the third major element of Said bin Sultan's
policy for the development of Zanzibar. The supply of ivory
coming to the coastal ports opposite the Arab ruler's island
entrepôt had to be made regular and certain. The Nyamwezi and
other African caravans coming from the interior could, and did,
perform a service in bringing ivory, but they were unable to
provide a stable enough supply to meet the expanding needs of
the resident foreign merchants of Zanzibar. Therefore Said bin
Sultan and his Arab and African subjects, financed by Indian
capital, began a steady and systematic penetration of the African
interior in search of ivory. Along with this penetration went an
allied development of the traffic in slaves, although this nefarious
trade was never of prime importance in the Nyamwezi areas. The
movement in search of ivory and slaves brought the Arabs into
the most distant reaches of east central Africa, to regions now
included in the modern African nations of Kenya, Somalia,
Uganda, Tanzania, Rwanda, Burundi, Mozambique, Malawi,
Zambia, and the Congo (Kinshasa). A few enterprising Arabs
even continued their travels right across the continent to Luanda
in Angola. Scattered through this immense area were bases established by the Arabs to serve as havens for protection and as
sources of provisions. Among the most important—its only rivals
among Arab centers were in the Congo—was the Arab establishment in the Nyamwezi chiefdom of Unyanyembe, located about
600 miles (by the winding caravan routes) from the East African
coast.

The trade flowing from this steady inland penetration drained
almost entirely into the Zanzibar entrepôt. Unlike the commercial
system in operation along the coast of western Africa, foreign
traders were not required to visit a series of small and often
competing ports. Said bin Sultan's efforts had been successful,
with trade goods arriving along the entire coast going largely
to Zanzibar because of its well-developed credit facilities and its

resident foreign merchants. Apart from this economic relationship, each of the participating coastal city-states under Said bin
Sultan's influence was left pretty much to its own devices for
political rule. If the suzerainty of the ruler of Zanzibar was
recognized, he had no great desire for additional interference,
nor did he really have the power to compel long-term obedience
without seriously harming the existing trading structure. Thus
the sultan was satisfied if the city-states accepted a few outward
signs of integration into the Zanzibari system. They included,
apart from the hoisting of the blood-red flag of Zanzibar, the
presence of Arab governors, permanent military garrisons (of a
very limited size), and—the real key to the system—the presence
of Indian representatives of the Customs Master to regulate commerce to and from Zanzibar.

The city-states of the coast in general found this loose system
congenial. Their harbors, many of them merely open tidal
beaches, were usually not satisfactory for the large vessels used
by long-distance traders, and, most important, each port by itself
did not normally draw sufficient trade to attract on its own permanent commercial agents. In addition, especially in the Somali
ports, such residents would have been forced to live in conditions
of great personal insecurity. Therefore, Zanzibar and the coastal
city-states came to a consensus of interests; if Said bin Sultan and
his successors did not unduly interfere in the way of life of the
coast, the inhabitants of the coast readily acknowledged the sultan as their ruler, permitting him to control the conditions of
their commerce. They clearly benefited from this control since
Said bin Sultan's policies greatly increased commercial activity.
The success of this consensus is proved by the relatively few times
that the rulers of Zanzibar felt compelled to use force to maintain
their position of leadership in the years before the European
seizure of East Africa.

THE ARABS AND THE NYAMWEZI AT UNYANYEMBE

The Nyamwezi regions directed most of their trade to the series
of small ports opposite Zanzibar, especially, as the nineteenth
century progressed, to the center of Bagamoyo, which because of

the Nyamwezi arrivals became the most active and prosperous of all the East African coastal city-states. Here, at the height of the caravan trading season, were found thousands of Nyamwezi and other African carriers of ivory. Some crossed over to Zanzibar, probably drawn by an overwhelming curiosity to see the most important city of East Africa, possessing as it did the region's only significant European community. The commercial transactions involving the visiting Africans, however, were carried on at Bagamoyo, as in other East African coastal ports, through a long series of bargaining negotiations between African seller and Indian buyer, both aided, for a price, by a coastal intermediary. Finally, when the prices of all commodities to be traded were established, ivory changed hands in return for cotton cloth, metal wire, firearms, gunpowder, and scores of items of lesser importance. Slaves were also carried along the routes to Bagamoyo and surrounding ports. Some were sold to African peoples along the way to the coast, such as to the Gogo, in return for ivory or provisions. Others changed owners at Bagamoyo and nearby, either for use in the Arab plantations of the coast, or for export to Zanzibar and beyond. But this human merchandise remained of secondary importance. Throughout the nineteenth century the principal slave-exporting center of East Africa remained in the southern regions of the sultan's dominions, which exploited an area reaching into modern Zambia, and especially centering the slave exports at the port of Kilwa Kivinje.

It was the venturesome Africans of the interior who had opened this regular contact between coastal and inland Africa, the Yao to the sultan's southern ports, the Nyamwezi to the ports opposite Zanzibar, and the Kamba to the northern ports. But it was not long before the subjects of Said bin Sultan were pushing inland along the newly opened routes. The Arab ruler himself dispatched exploratory caravans; he encouraged his subordinates to do likewise. It was a necessary step. Zanzibar was developing into one of the major ivory markets of the world: in 1859, three years after the death of Said bin Sultan, Zanzibar's ivory exports totaled 488,600 pounds. Even more pleasing to the island's ruler was the fact that East African ivory was of the highest quality. To ensure the continuation of this preeminence required a more regular method of securing ivory than that of independently arriving African caravans. The Nyamwezi and other Africans had their own motivations and schedules of operations, both likely to be interrupted by war, famine, epidemics, and other unsettling events, all calculated to upset the flow of profitable transactions in Said bin Sultan's island capital.

The course of inland Arab penetration led by the 1820's to the country of the Nyamwezi. Traditionally, the first arrivals were two Indian Muslims; one of them, Musa Mzuri, later became a leading member of the Arab community of Unyanyembe. But at first the main routes utilized by the Arabs did not have Unyamwezi as a principal objective. The traders instead struck to the southwest, to the territories of the Sangu (often called the Rori in nineteenth-century sources), principally because this course avoided the difficult territory of the Gogo through which passed the route opened by the first Nyamwezi arrivals at the coast. The Gogo peoples, organized into a series of independent political entities, without strong chiefly office, lived within a harsh environment which made caravan passage difficult. Food supplies were scarce and water sources were infrequent. And since the Gogo were numerous and warlike (the explorer Henry M. Stanley characterized them as "the Irish of Africa—clannish and full of fight"), they were easily able to dominate their limited resources. Caravans moving through their territories had little choice but to submit to the exactions demanded for passage. If not, they had to face a powerful people who could close off every available source of the necessities of life. Several reports survive of large Arab caravans which attempted to challenge these conditions; they all suffered severely, and some were completely destroyed. Clearly Ugogo was an area the Arabs preferred to avoid in favor of more peaceful routes. Nevertheless, during the 1840's, the Arabs were once more compelled to subject themselves to the rigors of travel among the Gogo. The Sangu, profiting from the firearms they had gained through their trade with the Arabs, became too unruly a people to live and travel among.

This circumstance, so harmful to the Arab goal of profitable trade, therefore led the Arabs to return to the more central homeland of the Nyamwezi. An indicative symptom of this change was the negotiations of 1839 between Arabs and Nyam-wezi in Zanzibar. The details of the deliberations are not known, nor are the identities of the particular Nyamwezi involved, but the concerned parties aimed at, and apparently succeeded in, establishing a system of mutual benefit which provided the Arabs security while they were in Nyamwezi territory. Another indica-tion of the increased amicable relationships between Zanzibar and Unyamwezi was reported by the French commercial agent, M. Loarer, in December 1848; he noted the arrival of a 2000-man Nyamwezi ivory caravan at the coastal center of Mbwamaji, op-posite Zanzibar, bearing gifts to exchange with Said bin Sultan.[8] Also, probably in the 1840's, Muhammad bin Juma, an important Arab, the father of Tippu Tip (of whom we shall hear more later), settled in the Nyamwezi chiefdom of Unyanyembe. This enterprising Arab, following a pattern which was repeated many times by his compatriots in the African interior, strengthened his position by marrying Karunde, a daughter of Unyanyembe's ruler, Fundikira I. At about the same time, other initially more important Arab commercial establishments were founded among the Nyamwezi of Msene (to the west of Mirambo's homeland, Uyowa) and of Puge (to the north of Unyanyembe).

But in the long run, Unyanyembe turned out to be the most important settlement for the furtherance of Arab interests. Its strategic central location, where many profitable caravan routes converged, gave that Nyamwezi chiefdom great advantages in drawing and maintaining an Arab community. Unyanyembe was also fertile enough to supply the needed provisions for the con-stantly multiplying number of Arab-led caravans. Moreover, Unyanyembe, an expanding state during the first half of the nineteenth century under its able rulers, Swetu and Fundikira I, recognized these advantages; its leaders worked actively to create an attractive and secure location for the Arab newcomers from the coast and Zanzibar. It was obviously good state policy to do so. The Nyamwezi remained a series of independent and regularly hostile competing chiefdoms. Whichever state had the Arabs

8 M. Loarer, "No. 1. Ile de Zanguebar. Organisation, Population, Poids, Mesures & Monnaies," O.I.5[23], Archives de l'Ancien Ministère de la France d'Outre Mer, Paris.

settled in its territory had the advantages of the services of a powerful ally, and of the new tools of warfare—firerams and gunpowder—which that ally had to supply its partners in order to safeguard its own interests. And if Unyanyembe had not utilized all its natural advantages to win over the Arabs, its Nyamwezi rivals would have welcomed the opportunity to move the Arabs into their own spheres. Thus in the 1850's when Puge became an unstable base for the Arabs because of warfare, they were encouraged to settle near Fundikira's center in the area which would later be known as Tabora.

Inevitably, the Arab settlers and their numerous armed African followers introduced a new, potentially disruptive force into the political life of the Nyamwezi chiefdoms in which they settled. The Arabs came to trade and their policies necessarily had to be designed to manipulate African societies in the manner which would provide them the greatest stability and profits. Arabs residing in a powerful African state like Buganda found it difficult, and at most times impossible, to exercise much local authority, but in the less firmly structured states of the Nyamwezi they had ample scope for successful intrigue. The principal weakness of the Nyamwezi states was their mechanism for the succession to the office of *ntemi* following the death of a ruler, a weakness common in many African political entities. In Unyanyembe, and among the rest of the Nyamwezi states, there was no previously designated and agreed-upon successor. All of those eligible under the laws of matrilineal succession, both males and females, were potential candidates to be considered for the office of *ntemi* by the deciding body, the ritual officers and greater headmen. The system was inherently unstable, with disappointed candidates often contesting their failure to secure the office in the years before the Arab arrival, and the Arabs then increased the instability by participating in the political process. The Arabs really had little alternative since their limited military strength did not allow an outright conquest. If they wanted to protect their profitable commercial position, the Arabs had to follow the only option available to them, the backing of one candidate favorable to their interests at each succession crisis. After the reign of Fundikira I, and until the days of German rule in

Tanzania, no *ntemi* of Unyanyembe was chosen without Arab support.

This new state of affairs manifested itself at the death of Fundikira I in 1858. His successor, Msabila (also called in the literature Mnwa Sele, Manwa Sera, and Msavila Kumagula), became *ntemi* with the backing of important members of the Arab community. The new Nyamwezi leader, a firm and resolute individual with decided military ability, was not a *ntemi* of the traditional kind. With Msabila the transformations that foreign commerce had made possible in that formerly largely ritual office became apparent. Rulers now recognized the opportunities open to them to manipulate for their profit the new forces in their communities, principally by striving to gain an increased share of the new kinds of non-perishable wealth, cloth, guns, and gunpowder, which allowed them to play an active political role within their states. The vital changes in Nyamwezi political life which allowed the rise of Mirambo were obviously under way.

Msabila set off on his fateful new course of policy by unilaterally imposing a tax upon all commodities entering Unyanyembe in Arab caravans. Later he justified his action to the British explorer, John Hanning Speke, with this reasonable explanation: "The Arabs were the only people who lived in my country exempt from taxation." The Arabs, however, whom Speke's superior, Richard F. Burton, reported about then as living "comfortably, and even splendidly" in Unyanyembe, reacted with moderation to the new impost, and if Msabila had held to his original policy without further incident, he might have succeeded by negotiations in securing his desired advantage. After all, to the Arabs a tax, if not too onerous, was far preferable to hostilities which might disrupt trade entirely. But Msabila became involved in difficulties with the Nyamwezi relatives of one of the leading Arab settlers in Unyanyembe, Muhammad bin Juma; some of them died in the affair. Thus provoked, Muhammad bin Juma and other Arabs, no doubt including many who were upset at Msabila's new tax, mobilized their considerable forces to support a rival candidate for the office of *ntemi*, Mkasiwa Kiyungi, one of Msabila's brothers. Msabila was unable to stand against their combined forces; in about 1860 their Arab-Nyamwezi combination drove him from his capital. Msabila remained an obdurate opponent, refusing to accept his deposition, and raiding and disrupting trade over the new few years. But despite at least one notable victory over an Arab-led expedition, when the well-known Arab leader Snay bin Amir was killed, Msabila was never able to regain his position as *ntemi* of Unyanyembe. The Arabs finally finished the lengthy affair by defeating and killing Msabila in 1865.

The Arabs had proved their strength in Unyanyembe. Msabila had demonstrated what course a *ntemi* of the 1860's might follow to modify his formerly political impotent position. His career also made it all too apparent that the Arabs were able to play upon the weaknesses of the political system of Unyanyembe to gain Nyamwezi allies for maintaining themselves in the forefront. Mkasiwa, a cautious, weak-willed, and later a physically unwell individual, was not henceforth disposed to challenge their interests. He was content, at least outwardly, to rule in alliance with the Arab residents, profiting thereby from their presence. It was not really a very degrading role for a Nyamwezi *ntemi;* Mkasiwa was free to devote himself to the duties of a traditional *ntemi,* leaving the satisfied Arabs to operate in a fashion roughly similar to that of the important headmen in the traditional Nyamwezi political process. As long as this situation continued, the Arabs could have no desire to attempt the removal of Mkasiwa from office.

The hostilities between Msabila and the Arabs, which naturally had had an adverse effect on the trade to Zanzibar, inevitably drew the attention of the island's authorities to Unyanyembe. Said bin Sultan's death had closed his long, seminal reign in 1856; he was succeeded by his son, Majid bin Said, a less innovative individual, who ruled until 1870. The new leader, as had his father before him, paid virtually no attention to the day-to-day affairs of his subjects residing in inland Africa. Majid's sole concern was that nothing should interfere with the normal commercial relationships between the coast and the interior. Msabila's stubborn resistance did just that, leading the sultan to an important decision. Majid, apparently reacting to the urgings of his Indian Customs Master, appointed a Zanzibari Arab to serve as his agent, or *liwali,* at Unyanyembe. Nineteenth-century European observers designated the *liwali* the governor of the Arab community among the Nyamwezi, but, as we shall see, he did little to live up to this description. There had never been such an official in the previous history of the Arab presence in Unyamwezi.

A well-known Arab, Said bin Salim al Lamki, received the appointment, thus becoming the titular head of the Unyanyembe Arabs, But there were serious limitations to the effective power of the new official. Said bin Salim was given no significant military force to uphold any unpopular directives he might receive from Zanzibar. Instead, in the way common to the Zanzibari political service, the *liwali* was expected to preside over the sultan's subjects and to enforce the wishes of his master through the mediums of extended discussion and persuasion. Said bin Salim did, however, have one potential strength which he could draw upon, the fact that he was as much a representative of the Customs Master of Zanzibar as of its ruler. Since many of the Arabs of the interior were deeply in debt to that official, or to other important Indians of Zanzibar, they normally had to heed the wishes of his representative. If not, these Arabs could never expect to return to Zanzibar without fear of imprisonment. In extreme cases, the family property in Zanzibar of an offending Arab could also be expropriated to control obedience or to discharge a debt. In view of these limitations on the day-to-day exercises of his office, the future difficulties of Said bin Salim with his fellow Arabs during the war with Mirambo of the early 1870's are easy to understand.

Said bin Salim al Lamki, the son of an Arab father, who had once been the sultan's *liwali* at Kilwa Kivinje, and an African or Malagash mother, was about fifty years of age when he became *liwali* in Unyanyembe. His first prominent role in East African affairs came following a period when he had served as a Zanzibari official at the minor Indian Ocean port of Sadani. Said bin Salim was designated by Majid bin Said as the chief Arab subordinate to the British explorers, Richard F. Burton and John H. Speke, on their 1857-58 expedition into the African interior. He accompanied them via Unyanyembe to Ujiji, the principal Arab center on Lake Tanganyika; his employers were the first Europeans to visit the lake. On the return journey to Zanzibar, Speke went on a side expedition, leaving Burton and Said bin Salim in Unyanyembe, which resulted in his reaching and naming Lake Victoria. Despite the strictures heaped upon Said bin Salim by the irascible Burton, Speke, on his return to Africa in 1860 with James A. Grant, hired his former Arab companion once more to conduct the caravan of his new expedition. Speke now sought to determine whether his bold guess that Lake Victoria was the source of the Nile was really true. But Said bin Salim's illness forced Speke to leave him to recuperate with the Arab community at Unyanyembe. It was probably this chance event, in 1861, giving the Arab the opportunity to increase his knowledge of the local Nyamwezi situation, which caused his later appointment as Zanzibari representative. Said bin Salim's most outstanding characteristic was his distaste for war; Speke had described him in 1859 as "a timid, though very gentlemenly creature," and the characterization was accurate. Said bin Salim came to Unyanyembe to represent the trading interests of Zanzibar; this only reinforced his natural proclivities. Such an attitude was not always a popular one among the Unyanyembe Arabs—even the missionary David Livingstone said in disgust, "though called a governor, he is only a Banian [Indian] trade agent."[9] And it was an attitude which slowly brought Said bin Salim into increasing disfavor when he had to deal with the major threat to Unyanyembe and the Arabs posed by Mirambo.

Thus by the beginning of the important decade of the 1870's, the balance of interests defining the relationships between the Arabs of Zanzibar and the Nyamwezi of Unyanyembe was stable. If all the details of the balance were not to the full satisfaction of all involved, at least the relationship then appeared the smoothest functioning system possible in face of the relative strength of the two groups. The Arab community was generally content since they maintained an effective control over the commercial affairs of the Nyamwezi state, while they possessed a safe base which normally provided an abundant supply of provisions. They had even agumented the supply of foodstuffs by supplementing the traditional Nyamwezi cultigens through the successful introduc-

9 Livingstone to Maclear, Nov. 17, 1871, in *Proceedings of the Royal Geographical Society*, 17 (1872-73), 71.

tion of the cultivation of rice, mangoes, and other coastal crops. And, finally, the Arabs had available for their service an abundant labor force of Nyamwezi males to work in the caravans they dispatched throughout east central Africa.

The Nyamwezi, on their side of the balance, also had little cause for complaint. Arab commerce, added to their own trading endeavors, enriched the Unyanyembe state. Under its complacent *ntemi*, Mkasiwa, it became the most powerful of all Nyamwezi states. The preceding conditions naturally brought full satisfaction to the Zanzibar authorities as they received regular and increasingly valuable amounts of ivory from the various areas connecting with the Unyanyembe commercial center. This prosperity, moreover, sharply increased during the 1860's when the Arabs utilizing the Unyanyembe route passed westward via Ujiji across Lake Tanganyika into the eastern Congo. There, in Manyema, the Arabs discovered the richest ivory-producing area yet exploited in the African interior, one where the politically and militarily impotent African inhabitants were unable to put any effective check on the Arab domination of the region. The Nyamwezi, working as the close allies of the Arabs, also shared the rewards. During the early 1880's, for example, a British missionary said: "In Unyamwezi . . . we find . . . many of the men possessing guns of their own, while they wear fine clothes, the produce of India, as under-garments, with long *Kanzus* (shirt-like articles of dress) over all. All the men are dressed decently in some kind of cloth or other. The women . . . generally wear fine coloured handkerchiefs, prints, blue or white calico. It is only in some little out of the way village that we ever find persons still wearing the skins of animals."[10] But if the Nyamwezi of Unyanyembe and the Arabs, both in Unyanyembe and in Zanzibar, were satisfied with this profitable arrangement, other Nyamwezi were increasingly restive about their secondary position. The redoubtable Mirambo was ready to enter the competitions for the wealth of the African interior and to challenge the Arab domination of the most lucrative trade route of east central Africa.

---

[10] W. Hutley, "Mohammedanism in Central Africa," in Hutley to Thompson, Sept. 12, 1881, Central Africa, 1881-1882, CCWM.

II

MIRAMBO'S EARLY YEARS

MIRAMBO'S YOUTH

AMONG THE MANY small and unimportant Nyamwezi chiefdoms which developed away from the heady atmosphere of the African-Arab commercial center at Unyanyembe was Uyowa, located in the curve of the Igombe River about sixty miles to the northwest of Unyanyembe on the caravan route to the Lake Tanganyika port of Ujiji. Mirambo in his later life described his homeland as a very insignificant entity: at his accession as its *ntemi* Uyowa contained, he estimated, a population of about 4000 Nyamwezi spread out among six village centers. There is little available information to distinguish Uyowa from the many other similarly insignificant Nyamwezi states existing in the early nineteenth century. Its population must have concerned itself with the normal Nyamwezi endeavors, in agriculture and stock raising, in short- and long-distance trade, and in the continuing, but not too damaging, military rivalries with other Nyamwezi states

Sometime around 1840—the exact date is unknown—Nyakashi, principal wife of *ntemi* Kasanda of Uyowa, gave birth to a son. As was often the custom, the child was named after his paternal grandfather (the uncle of *ntemi* Kasanda) and his material grandfather. Called Mbula Mtelya, he would be better known in later years as Mirambo (in this study only the latter name will be used). Mirambo was born in the Nyamwezi chiefdom of Ukune, near Uyowa. Nyakashi was the issue of its ruling dynasty and it

was customary among Nyamwezi women to attempt bearing their
first child at their parents' home. Nothing specific is known of
Mirambo's early years. But there is no reason to believe that
his upbringing was significantly different from that of any
other male member of a contemporary Nyamwezi ruling family
since, with the Nyamwezi lack of a fixed system of political
succession, there was no certain indication that Mirambo would
ever be the ruler of Uyowa.

Once the first years of childhood were completed, Mirambo
would have experienced, along with his age mates, the course of
education provided to Nyamwezi youths from which they progressively absorbed the skills needed for the adult world of Unyamwezi. Mirambo doubtlessly participated in the male agricultural tasks, in the care of livestock, in war games, and in sundry
group endeavors such as house building. Other learning came
from the former Nyamwezi custom of having special huts in each
village for young men and for unmarried girls, where there was
considerable freedom in sexual matters. During his adolescent
years Mirambo almost certainly joined his age mates in caravan
life, thus demonstrating his manhood in the way common to any
other growing Nyamwezi youth. It was not at all uncommon for
youths of the royal Nyamwezi lines to do this. Fundikira I of
Unyanyembe, for example, first learned of his selection as *ntemi*
of Unyanyembe while serving as a carrier in a caravan. Msiri,
the outstanding Nyamwezi ruler of nineteenth-century Katanga,
is also said to have served in caravans during his youth. However, it does not appear likely that Mirambo ever visited the
East African coast during this period of his life since he made
no reference to such an unusual experience during his later life.

Looking back from Mirambo's later career, the youth manifestly must have had significant experience in learning the techniques of nineteenth-century Nyamwezi warfare. It is probably
significant that his father, *ntemi* Kasanda, was often described in
the period after Mirambo's rise to prominence as the able leader
of a band of warriors, while nothing else of much importance
was said concerning him. Any warfare Kasanda or his subordinates acting in his name participated in would have been waged
on a very small scale, really amounting to no more than raiding,

which brought limited rewards in booty to the ruler of the small state of Uyowa. But during the course of these sporadic hostilities Mirambo must have absorbed, far more efficiently than most of his Nyamwezi contemporaries, the new tactics of warfare introduced into the Nyamwezi regions by the Ngoni. This dynamic African group, originally stemming from the Nguni-speaking peoples of southern Africa, mounted one of the most disruptive, and most influential, invasions of nineteenth-century east central Africa. Because of difficulties with the harsh Zulu leader, Shaka, the Ngoni had set off northward under their leader, Zwangendaba, early in the century. They were one of the most successful indigenous military forces that Black Africa has known, utilizing the effective military tactics perfected by Shaka, and relying upon the disciplined use of their broad shields and short stabbing spears, to bring them victory. Youths entered the military regiments of Shaka, and the Ngoni, there to remain until their leader allowed them retirement and marriage. All advancement, as well as the individual warrior's share of the booty gained from victory, depended upon the leader. The influence of the Ngoni in nineteenth-century Tanzania was immense, and they played a vital role in influencing Mirambo's career.

One small section of this martial African people arrived in the Unyamwezi region, where they were locally known as the Tuta, at just about the time during the 1850's that Mirambo was beginning to join in the pursuits of adulthood. The Hehe and other East African peoples profited militarily from the Ngoni example; Mirambo did likewise, but his exact relationship to the Ngoni during his youth is unclear. One explanation, supposedly emanating from Mirambo himself, was often advanced by nineteenth-century European observers who sought to explain Mirambo's military skills. They related that Mirambo, either as a volunteer or as a war captive, had lived for some time among the Ngoni, thus learning their military ways through participation in the Ngoni campaigns. The main proofs for the assertion were Mirambo's military tactics, clearly similar to those of the Ngoni, and his ability to speak the Ngoni language. Nevertheless a stay among the Ngoni was not really necessary to explain Mirambo's later successes. Once the Ngoni were present in Unyamwezi their example was there for all to observe or experience, whether as neutral bystanders, allies, or unfortunate victims. Mirambo was certainly not the only Nyamwezi leader to profit by their techniques. As for Mirambo's knowledge of the Ngoni language, it is easily explained by the geographical proximity of these Nyamwezi and Ngoni fellow speakers of Bantu languages. But however Mirambo gained his knowledge of Ngoni military methods, the result was clear enough. This forceful young man, as skilled as any other Nyamwezi in that group's traditional practice of warfare, added to this experience the knowledge to allow the eventual creation of a disciplined African fighting force able to succeed in most of its combats against the more common irregular and often very unorganized military bodies that were then current in east central Africa.

About 1858 *ntemi* Kasanda of Uyowa died. If his state then followed the rules of matrilineal succession, which it probably did, Mirambo should not normally have come to power as Kasanda's successor. Two explanations are possible. Either Kasanda had no eligible, or capable, nephews, and thus Mirambo was designated ruler, or Mirambo, perhaps already possessing a reputation, and a following, as a war leader, seized the office by force. The latter procedure was common enough in the frequently turbulent succession struggles of the mid-nineteenth-century Nyamwezi. The actual events unfortunately remain unknown. Apart from the few oral accounts stemming from Mirambo, and from those who accepted his legitimacy—and in view of his later triumphs, this was the prevailing opinion—there are no written accounts of any value for this early period. Richard F. Burton passed through Uyowa in 1857; he reported nothing of unusual interest. During an 1861 visit John H. Speke was impressed at the total mobilization of the chiefdom for a campaign; unfortunately, he gave no details about Uyowa's *ntemi*. Perhaps Mirambo was already at work, but Speke's reference is not precise enough for any meaningful conclusions. The same lack of detailed information persists during the remainder of the 1860's. In the words of the famous Arab trader and raider of central Africa, Tippu Tip, during the course of the Msabila struggles at Unyanyembe, "And at this time no one knew about Mirambo."

But if the Arabs did not know about the vigorous ruler of Uyowa, Mirambo was manifestly making an impact upon his African neighbors. In not too distant Ulyankulu, a small Nyamwezi chiefdom, the royal line was related to Mirambo. *Ntemi* Kasele of Ulyankulu was a grandfather of Mirambo. According to tradition, when Kasele was old and blind the young Mirambo, not yet *ntemi* of Uyowa, became a favorite of the Ulyankulu ruler because of his considerate treatment of his elderly and infirm relative. This solicitude pleased Kasele all the more since his nephews, Kasimana and Mkindo, who were expected to succeed to his office, neglected and mistreated their uncle. Despite Kasele's affection for Mirambo, however, the rules of matrilineal succession prevailed at his death and first Kasimana, and then Mkindo, became *ntemi* of Ulyankulu. Mirambo, fast rising in military strength, moved to take the rule of the chiefdom in about 1860. There are no accounts of any opposition to the usurpation. Mirambo later estimated that his new possession of Ulyankulu was composed of five large settlements with a total population of 6000.

MIRAMBO, NTEMI OF URAMBO

Then, flushed with the success of his past triumphs, the young warrior *ntemi* adopted the name of Mirambo (many Nyamwezi took different names at important stages of their lives). The name means "corpses," signalizing that the Nyamwezi leader through his many victorious battles was indeed "a maker of corpses." Uyowa and Ulyankulu henceforth were known as Urambo, the country of Mirambo, and despite their limited size, with about a ten-mile radius and a combined population of around 10,000, they served as the active center of the largest Nyamwezi political entity ever created.

Unhampered by this small beginning, Mirambo, when he appeared on the greater East African scene, had behind him a people and a state fully and efficiently organized to support the rigors of the almost continuous warfare their *ntemi* engaged in. Such organization was a very rare phenomenon in nineteenth-century east central Africa, notably among Mirambo's rivals

within the Nyamwezi regions. It largely explains the reasons for
Mirambo's continuing series of military triumphs. The first essential requirement of this fighting organization was a secure home
base, Urambo, well able to supply the men required for campaigning and to provide the agricultural surpluses needed to
support Mirambo's men during their military endeavors. There
never was any doubt about the strength of Mirambo's home area;
united behind their *ntemi,* the people of Urambo faced no serious invasions or other disruptions once Mirambo's career was
under way.

The military force which Mirambo assembled proved to be a
significant innovation among the Nyamwezi. The traditional
methods of warfare involved the calling-up of able-bodied men
in a chiefdom through the authority of the important headmen
of that state. Without strong control at the center of the chiefdom, it was at best an imperfect mechanism. Mirambo, far removed from the weak authority of the traditional ritual *ntemi,*
freed himself from the uncertainties of irregularly called levies
by creating what was very close to a permanent standing army.
He utilized African warriors from areas other than Urambo to
buttress the strength of his indigenous followers. Their combined
forces were known to nineteenth-century East Africa as *ruga-ruga*
(according to Aylward Shorter it means "a young, unmarried
soldier"). Within their ranks were adventurous individuals who
were ready to volunteer their skilled services to any leader whose
utilization of their military prowess brought them continuous
victory and its resulting spoils. Thus the *ruga-ruga* originated
from many different tribal groupings, but above all they were
drawn from the ranks of venturesome Nyamwezi, many of whom
had traveled to the coast to earn the requisite amount for the
purchase of the necessary firearms for starting their career. By
the 1870's the *ruga-ruga,* serving a wide range of African and
Arab leaders, were an active, disruptive force operating to the
detriment of peaceful populations throughout the extended area
between the East African coast and the Congo River. It is this
use of "mercenaries" by Mirambo which has caused several
writers, notably the British scholar Alison Smith, to describe him,
and several other roughly similar leaders of his generation, as

warlords. The term is striking, but the implications it carries from non-African milieus may hide more than was originally intended. Mirambo was not merely a military leader dependent chiefly upon mercenaries. He was above all the ruler of a well-functioning Nyamwezi state, and this position provided Mirambo's main source of strength.

Joined to the "mercenaries" and men of Urambo were other Africans whom Mirambo recruited from the areas he had defeated and then absorbed into his growing state. Mirambo impressed promising young individuals from each subjugated area to bring them up and train them as fighting men. Together, all these warriors from the various foreign and domestic sources, following the Ngoni pattern, had to remain unmarried and devoted only to warfare until their fighting career was over. Then Mirambo permitted them to marry and he rewarded them with slaves and land according to the extent of their faithful service. These men provided Mirambo with the tools for victory. They lived for fighting, nothing else, and as Mirambo's career developed, this proved both a strength and a weakness for Mirambo's state: a machine designed for warfare can never be left idle for too long. All of the warriors resided within easy call of Mirambo's capital and remained ready for immediate mobilization. And once in battle array the warriors must have made a very disquieting impression upon their intended opponents. Wearing at times a blood red cape, with their long, uncut hair worked with ochre, and often charging into battle fired by the smoking of bhang (Indian hemp) and loudly singing martial airs, their psychological impact was immense.

Mirambo's men carried firearms, usually muzzle loaders, although ammunition was at times scarce owing to the restrictive policies of the ruler of Zanzibar, but such arms were not a vital necessity for victory, a fact proved by other martial East African peoples, including the formidable Masai and Hehe, who usually triumphed over their enemies without them. The poor quality of the trade guns available to Africans was also a factor against their effective use, one British missionary remarking in 1876, "I hope I shall never be near one of them which fired; I am sure a bit of gas pipe would be a safer arm and equally destructive to

the firer."[1] Consequently, many Africans using firearms, including Mirambo's men, often merely fired one shot when a battle
began, then reverting to traditional, and more effective, weapons
for close-quarter combat. The vital elements essential for victory
were not firearms but disciplined organization and inspired
leadership. Mirambo provided both. He had created a personal
army, one of the finest fighting machines of his region, which
was loyal only to him, not to the entity of Urambo. As long as
Mirambo lived his men would willingly follow him. If ever this
force was not numerous enough Mirambo sought alliances with
other neighboring martial African peoples. The Ngoni in particular were often allies of the Urambo ruler. But such allies,
however necessary in any one campaign, were dangerous friends,
not always to be relied upon, since they fought for booty alone.
They were a useful adjunct, but Mirambo's main strength came
always from his own personal followers.

Mirambo's campaigns usually followed the same general pattern. Once the season of rains was finished, with the crops harvested and the paths fit for speedy travel, Mirambo, who was
no traditional stay-at-home *ntemi,* led his forces in person,
marching during his younger years at their van. Estimates vary
concerning the size of the Nyamwezi leader's war machine; on
one particularly significant campaign, observers reported forces
numbering up to 7000 men, but armies of less than half that size
were probably used in Mirambo's more normal, briefer ventures.
Once off against the enemy, Mirambo's tactic was to hit his foes
by surprise, usually at dawn, so that the stockaded village under
attack could be entered before any well-organized resistance
emerged. It was necessary to fight in this way since Nyamwezi
strongholds, if properly fortified and supplied with adequate
water and provisions, were very difficult to take by African
armies fighting without benefit of artillery. Long sieges were
equally difficult for an invading force of any size since they soon
exhausted the available provisions in the nearby areas, while the
primitive methods of transport precluded their conveying large

---

[1] O'Neill to Wright, July 12, 1876, C.A6/M1, Church Missionary Society
Archives, London [hereafter CMS].

amounts of provisions from more distant sources. Mirambo's *ruga-ruga,* once inside the opposing village, killed most, if not all, of the adult males who resisted them, and even at times those individuals who did not resist, until victory was assured. Both the tactics of warfare and the composition of Mirambo's army clearly reflect the influence of the Ngoni. But Mirambo was not merely a war leader without ideas of his own beyond the Ngoni influences.

With victory, Mirambo immediately took steps which marked him as more than the conquering leader of a disciplined band of plunderers. He appointed a new ruler for the occupied center, the former leader having usually been killed during the hostilities; the decision leading to the appointment normally followed discussions with those surviving officials responsible for the traditional mechanisms of succession. Often, the individual who would have succeeded following the normal deliberations after the predecessor's death was chosen. But now this individual entered office as a subordinate to Mirambo; he had to play a supportive role in Mirambo's state, supplying, when called upon, men and other resources for campaigns. To help ensure loyalty Mirambo not infrequently married a relation of the new ruler; he also took hostages from the royal line to Urambo. The conquered center and its new chief, with some of Mirambo's troops left behind to observe their conduct, were doubtless not always happy at the turn of events. Nevertheless the ruler did owe his succession to Mirambo; any disobedience of the required norms of conduct would cost him his position and probably his life. Obedience, conversely, brought a share in the booty of Mirambo's campaigns and the enjoyment of the peaceful prosperity that Mirambo's fearsome reputation brought to his dominions. Since, until his very last years, Mirambo had few rivals who had any chance of overthrowing his dominant position, the choice for Mirambo's subordinates was obvious.

Not all of Mirambo's dependents came from conquered territory. As his battle fame grew, so that all, even the most distant, or secure, African leaders had to think of an eventual attack, many neighboring Nyamwezi *ntemis* thought it better to make an advantageous alliance before any hostilities came. One such

typical decision was made by Majembe Gana, *ntemi* of the nearby Nyamwezi state of Uyui. Mirambo, while raiding near Uyui,
sent its *ntemi* one hundred hoes and one hundred bullets—he
had to choose between peace and war. Majembe Gana, the name
means "one hundred hoes," quickly made his choice. From that
time on he remained a loyal ally to Mirambo, later explaining
to a questioning missionary his participation in a campaign of
little personal interest to him by saying simply that it was better
to do so than to oppose Mirambo and thus to lose his state.[2] In
view of the alternatives, the resulting demands of such allied
rulers, mostly for fighting men, were not unduly onerous, and
the allied *ntemis* were for the most part left free within their
own states to act in the manner they chose.

In evaluating the factors that contributed to the development
of the state and of military strength, one can argue that Mirambo
was one of the most successful of the rulers of east central Africa.
His initial power base was insignificant and he exploited the
opportunities opened by the joining of the worlds of the East
African coast and interior. Mirambo had no personal experience
of the Muslim-influenced coastal world dominated by Zanzibar
and in diplomatic and commercial relations with India, Europe,
and the United States. At most he might have met and conversed
with a few Arabs or coastal Africans who as traders visited his
territories. But this world of the coast was changing the world
around Mirambo because of the increasing presence of visiting
traders. Firearms, gunpowder, cotton cloth, mechanical objects,
knowledge of new matters that struck at the traditional patterns
of Nyamwezi life, all were there for the more astute of the African leaders to seize upon for the advancement of themselves and
their peoples. A large part of Mirambo's greatness came from his
receptivity to the new objects and ideas. How this receptivity
germinated we do not know, but clearly it was there, and in
Mirambo, East Africa had one of its first leaders ready to break
from the comfortable but constraining limits of the traditional
African patterns of life to meet, and to attempt to master, the

2 C. T. Wilson and R. W. Felkin, *Uganda and the Egyptian Sudan* (London, 1882), I, 134-36; Copplestone to Hutchinson, Oct. 27, 1880, G3.A6/o1,
CMS.

new world opening before all East Africans. If Mirambo was a warlord, so were the other dynamic East African leaders of the nineteenth century, even including the powerful Mutesa I of Buganda (see Chapter VIII). Both of these masterful men, Mirambo and Mutesa, were traditional rulers utilizing new techniques and personnel to maximize their power. In their own way they were following the example set by Peter the Great of Imperial Russia during an earlier century. For Mirambo, the process led to one of the two most significant events of his career, his important decision to challenge the Unyanyembe-Arab near monopoly of the ivory trade between Unyamwezi and Zanzibar.

MIRAMBO THE MAN

In 1870 Mirambo was in the full vigor of his adult life, ready to face the stern moral and physical challenges of war, while at the same time being prepared to deal with the beginnings of the significant European penetration into his region of Africa. What kind of man was he? The surviving illustrations of Mirambo, added to the descriptions given by the visitors of the 1870's and 1880's (usually colored by their emotions at the moment of contact), give us a relatively clear indication of his physical appearance. Mirambo was a very imposing man, a little under six feet tall, strongly built without being stout. Normally he dressed very simply, much like his subjects, often surprising Europeans who expected so powerful and famous a sovereign to appear in special garb. Around 1880, for example, his normal dress, according to the missionary Ebenezer Southon, was an "old fustian coat" worn over traditional garments. At times, however, Mirambo did allow himself the luxury of wearing the raiment common to the Muslim East African coast, a practice followed by many of the inland African rulers of his day. Henry M. Stanley met him in 1876 in this dress; he wore an Arab coat, tarbush, slippers, and carried an Arab sword. The special apparel was not necessary; Mirambo carried his regal bearing within himself.

His strong frame was essential enough for a war leader; far more important was the rigor of his intellect. Mirambo stood ready to hear and consider all new ideas; he might accept them or reject them, he might act wisely or foolishly after pondering them, but the ideas did receive careful consideration. Mirambo seldom allowed his emotions to break through an impassive outer mien; nevertheless he appeared to almost all who came to him in friendship as a frank, kindly, and courteous individual, a man of inherently noble character. When a decision was needed, however difficult, Mirambo made it quickly, and then went on to carry out the choice efficiently. Unusual among African leaders, and leaders of other nationalities, Mirambo, reacting against what he described as the excesses of his earlier years, did not drink. He said simply to one missionary, "I could not do all my business and well govern my people if I drank pombe (African beer)."

As befitting the leader of warriors that he was, Mirambo was used to ready obedience, and he used force to govern his potentially unruly subjects. For example, when one day a subordinate village refused to send representatives to a levy he had called, Mirambo seized by a surprise move three of the guilty village leaders and had them executed. When a missionary, trying to tame the African chief, expressed his conviction that his queen, Victoria, would never have acted in so harsh a manner, Mirambo was unimpressed, merely replying that this was the only way in which he could govern his diverse peoples. Or, in another instance, when Mirambo had given his usual orders that no one was to molest a passing European-led caravan, a youth was caught stealing from it. When the caravan had left—Mirambo was aware of the susceptibilities of Europeans—he personally executed the offender for violating his directives. This was not an exceptional act; it was the normal way Mirambo kept order among the warriors and citizens of Urambo. And even Europeans could experience this underlying fierceness if they pushed the outwardly amiable chieftain too far. Another missionary, attempting to retrieve some firearms once belonging to a recently deceased member of his society, had to admit that it was "a task something like getting back so many lumps of beef from a lion—a little tamed perhaps but still a lion."[3]

3 Hore to Whitehouse, Dec. 5, 1883, Central Africa, 1883-1884, CCWM.

This strong African personality told a visitor, the Belgian officer Jerome Becker, that he was the "most grand Sultan of Africa," fully believing it was true. It was the measure of the man that before the visitor left Urambo he was usually in agreement with his African host.

III

MIRAMBO VERSUS THE ARABS

"MIRAMBO'S CAREER IS only understandable in terms of his opposition to the Arabs," concluded the British anthropologist R. G. Abrahams in his valuable study on the Nyamwezi. This perceptive generalization does not adequately explain the course of Mirambo's entire career, particularly after 1875, but with it Abrahams does arrange the stage for the events of the early 1870's in Unyamwezi. We have attempted to analyze how Mirambo's creation of the chiefdom of Urambo, including Uyowa, Ulyankulu, and a steadily augmented list of other incorporated or allied areas, had given him a secure niche in the continuing Nyamwezi power struggle. But it was by necessity a position of strictly limited strength. Unyanyembe, with its quiet and faceless ruler Mkasiwa, and its active Arab settlement avidly busy in attempting to control the available wealth either present in or passing through the chiefdom, easily stood supreme among the many Nyamwezi states. Under Mkasiwa's uninspired direction there was no significant impetus for the conquest of other Nyamwezi chiefdoms from Unyanyembe; nevertheless the strength of that state was formidable, and the abundant wealth its citizens gained from its Arab relationship was jealously apparent to all. To an ambitious and rising Nyamwezi leader like Mirambo, the next step in his expansionist policy was clearly the mounting of a direct challenge to Unyanyembe's priority. In brief, if Mirambo wanted to dominate Unyamwezi and the surrounding dependent regions successfully, he had to draw Unyanyembe's Arab traders to work for him as the most important Nyamwezi leader. This could be done either by the Arabs' voluntarily accepting Mirambo's right to impose new conditions regulating the Arab-Nyamwezi trading relationship, or by his coercing the Arab community through military might to abandon Unyanyembe for Urambo.

In retrospect, particularly in view of the disruption of Arab commerce which was soon accomplished by Mirambo, a peaceful coming to terms with the Urambo *ntemi* might have proved a wise policy for the Arabs. Even as early as the beginning of the 1870's this approach should have been a possibility meriting serious consideration by the Arab community of Unyanyembe. If, as is commonly asserted by many scholars working in East African history, the Arabs were little interested in outright political domination over the African peoples they lived and traded with, it could have been far wiser for them to abandon the amenable but weak ruler of Unyanyembe, who had virtually no influence outside of his own territories, in favor of the rising star of Mirambo. The Arabs would have continued in possession of a secure trading base, either at Urambo or at a Unyanyembe made dependent to Mirambo. There were potential candidates enough for Mkasiwa's office to have allowed the placing of a new ruler in Unyanyembe owing his position to the continued good will of the Urambo *ntemi,* and the Arabs would thereby have gained a formidable individual in Mirambo to arrange terms with. The unshakable Arab monopoly of the needed commodities issuing from Zanzibar would have guaranteed their position of value to Mirambo; he in return would have provided the Arabs secure conditions of trade in an ever-increasing area of eastern Africa.

But policies, then or now, are seldom made in the abstract, with a realistic evaluation of the strengths and weaknesses stemming from a major innovative decision. The various individuals directing the destinies of the Arabs and Nyamwezi of Unyanyembe had a very precise opinion concerning Mirambo's character. To them he was a volatile war leader, a chief not to be trusted as an ally in their effort to draw the greatest revenues from the African interior. A satisfactory and profitable status quo is difficult to change for men possessing only ordinary minds. *Ntemi* Mkasiwa was, after all, a loyal and proven ally to the Arabs; he was not at all likely to vary what the Arabs considered the satisfactory balance of interests in Unyanyembe. And the nominal head of the Arab community, the *liwali* Said bin Salim, was the most cautious of men, certainly not the type of individual who would shake a system accepted by nearly all of the principal Arab residents of Mkasiwa's state. The existing trade was profitable; that, above all, was the reason which justified Said bin Salim's continued presence in Unyanyembe to his Arab and Indian superiors in Zanzibar. Nevertheless, if all decisions concerning Mirambo had been left to Said bin Salim alone, he probably would have attempted to come to terms with the ruler of Urambo, in spite of the difficulty of this approach. Stanley has recounted that Mirambo refused to negotiate with Said bin Salim unless the *liwali* guaranteed that the Arab community would come to his aid against Mkasiwa. However difficult to achieve, almost any arrangement the *liwali* made with Mirambo would have raised little opposition from Zanzibar as long as Mirambo's terms, or any compromise based upon them, worked to the benefit of all segments of the Zanzibari state by increasing the amount of commodities flowing from and to Zanzibar's bustling market.

This logical solution, however, had no chance of gaining acceptance in Unyanyembe at the beginning of the decade of the 1870's. It took some time even for Said bin Salim to be convinced by events of the weaknesses of the hitherto successful Arab policy. And most of the *liwali's* important cohorts were naturally satisfied with the existing system based upon a compliant Nyamwezi dynasty, especially since it was a compliance which had been achieved through the long and costly hostilities—due to the hindrance of trade—leading to the death of Msabila. To the Arab community at large, Mirambo was a little-known individual; what they did know about his warlike characteristics only increased their basic antagonism toward him as a man who might interfere with their established patterns of procedure.

Also, by its very nature, the Arab community of Unyanyembe was markedly ill-fitted for the making of major decisions involving change of the established order. Said bin Salim had very limited authority or influence apart from the strengths he drew from his financial ties to Zanzibar, and even they would not sustain his role as *liwali* if he lost the confidence of his fellow Arab residents. And although all of the Arabs recognized Said bin Salim as the sultan's *liwail,* several of their number regarded themselves as being equally qualified to share in directing the affairs of their community in Unyanyembe. The Arabs of Oman were among the most independent-natured peoples in the world; their descendents living in Africa, as the rulers of Zanzibar were all too well aware, had lost nothing of their Arabian heritage. Thus Said bin Salim worked with a very imperfectly structured system for the decision making necessary to face the threat posed by the unified leadership of Urambo.

Three of the most notable Arab leaders involved with the *liwali* in the oncoming hostilities with Mirambo were Khamis bin Abdulla, and the two brothers, Shaykh bin Nasibu and Abdulla bin Nasibu. Khamis bin Abdulla, a young man of full Omani Arab descent, was a persuasive speaker, demonstrably capable of firing his listeners with confidence before a battle. To Henry Stanley, who regarded him as the embodiment of all the Arab virtues, Khamis bin Abdulla was "a bold and brave man, ever ready to stand up for the privileges of the Arabs, and their rights to pass through any country for legitimate trade." It was these qualities which catapulted Khamis bin Abdulla to the head of the Arab community in the first hostilities with Mirambo. The Nasibu brothers, of Arab and African ancestry, were far more influential in the normal affairs of the Unyanyembe community than the young and mercurial Khamis bin Abdulla. Shaykh bin Nasibu, who had served his sultan on diplomatic tasks in the interior, had important connections in Zanzibar, while in Unyanyembe he was universally regarded by the Arabs as one of the wisest members of their community. When Tippu Tip spoke of Shaykh bin Nasibu in later years, he concisely described that Arab's position: "His powers had in the past been very great, greater even than the Wali, who couldn't do anything without his sanction." Abdulla bin Nasibu, who subsequently became the Arab leader Mirambo most disliked, complemented his brother's grave mien and quiet wisdom. He was one of the foremost Arab warriors of the interior, earning through his many victories the name which all gave him, Kissessa, the "Valiant." And by using his victories to win supporters, through a very generous distribution of the spoils to his followers, Abdulla bin Nasibu had acquired a large and devoted following in Unyanyembe. He was not in Unyamwezi when hostilities with Mirambo began, but he quickly returned to exercise an important influence in the subsequent events. These three Arabs were determined men, standing on the simple principle that if African leaders came forward to challenge their system, then these Africans must be defeated. Moreover, this had to be done severely, both to serve as an example to the vanquished challengers, plus any other aspiring Africans, and to provide substantial booty for the Arabs' followers—including the *ruga-ruga* within their ranks— whose loyalty ensured continued domination.

The leadership within the Arab community of Unyanyembe remained divided, even though some of the leaders discussed here were replaced by other Arabs, through the end of Mirambo's career to the downfall of the last independent *ntemi* of Unyanyembe, Isike, in 1893. Thus there was no serious thought of compromise with Mirambo among the leaders of the Arab community. Since the ruler of Urambo similarly had no thought of ending his expansionist policies, war became inevitable.

THE WAR, 1871-75

When major hostilities began between Mirambo and the Unyanyembe-Arab coalition in 1871, the underlying reasons for the bitter struggle to come were not very clear to contemporary observers, either in the African interior or in Zanzibar. Mirambo was caricatured by most of them as merely another in that regrettably long line of unruly barbarian leaders who were always attempting to disturb the Zanzibar commercial system for their own immediate profit, without having any creative substitute plans for restructuring the order they attacked. Thus when fighting ensued, simple causes were provided to explain its origin. Sundry observers often advanced a story that Mirambo, while

still a young man, had been unjustifiably struck by an Arab
while serving in his caravan, this engendering in the fierce African youth a deep, life-long hatred for all Arabs. Therefore, the
prevailing opinion makers continued, Mirambo, after a long
career as a successful bandit leader, had at last received the one
final stimulus for his hatred for Arabs, and war followed. There
are various accounts describing the exact incident which broke
the uneasy quiet between Mirambo and the Arabs. In one ren-
dition Mirambo had advanced a considerable lot of ivory on
credit to an Arab trader who continually refused to reimburse
the Urambo *ntemi* for his merchandise. When the Unyanyembe
Arab community refused to help Mirambo to secure his just debt,
he lost his patience, seizing a caravan belonging to an Arab
partner of the original offender to recoup his loss. Or, another
observer explained, a passing Arab caravan leader had once
made very insulting remarks to Mirambo. The enraged African
chief bided his time until a fugitive slave from the guilty Arab
fled to Urambo for asylum. Mirambo granted the slave his protection. The Arab master then sent a representative to argue the
case with Mirambo, to no avail, but while in Urambo the Arab
delegate committed the great offence of seducing one of Mirambo's young wives. Finally, some Arabs asserted that Mirambo had
halted an Arab caravan passing through his territories on the
way to Ujiji, compelling its leader to pay an exceptionally onerous *hongo,* but then refusing to let the caravan proceed on its
journey, instead forcing the disgruntled Arabs to return to
Unyanyembe. Depending upon the political bias of the recounter
of such tales (and there are also several other related accounts),
then either Mirambo or the Arabs attacked, and bore the responsibility for the major war beginning in 1871.

All of these several explanations, even if one did truthfully
depict the actual incident which set the opposing forces fighting,
were basically irrelevant to the real causes of the war. Mirambo
had no love for the Arabs in general, but he realistically valued
them for the same reasons almost every other African ruler did—
their functions as the bringers of the commodities of the modern
non-African world. Even during the years of warfare with the
Arabs of Unyanyembe, Mirambo continued to deal with indi-

vidual Arabs who refused to heed the directives of the leaders
of that community for materials necessary to sustain his war
effort. Mirambo had not been swayed by an irrational hatred
of the Arabs; he had instead rationally taken a fateful policy
decision to fight and defeat the Arabs of Unyanyembe. The stakes
were great. If he won, Mirambo would become master of the
main trade route to the rich ivory regions of central Africa, and,
consequently, one of the most powerful, and wealthy, men of his
era. The simple version of Mirambo's motives is worth the telling only because it was accepted as reality in the 1870's by many
of the Arab leaders and those they met with, now including
Europeans, in Unyanyembe and in Zanzibar, thus long delaying
between the contending belligerents any meaningful negotiations
leading to a settlement.

A more detailed analysis of Mirambo's career becomes possible
with the onset of this struggle for control of trade, aided by the
surviving observations of a steadily increasing flow of European
and American visitors to East Africa. In June 1871 an impatient
and imperious reporter for James Gordon Bennett's mass circula-
tion daily newspaper, the *New York Herald,* arrived in Unyanyembe. Henry Morton Stanley, then thirty years of age and still
relatively inexperienced in matters African, was en route to Lake
Tanganyika for his momentous meeting at Ujiji with that Vic-
torian ideal of an African explorer, Dr. David Livingstone. The
Arabs of Unyanyembe received Stanley's large, well-led, and
strongly armed caravan with even more than their usual generous hospitality, setting for themselves the task of winning Stanley's support in the fight against Mirambo. The American star
reporter, not one to miss a good story, even if participation in a
war was involved, was easily convinced. And Stanley had other
reasons, convincing at least to him, that justified his aiding the
Arabs. He had spent about three months in reaching Unyanyembe, a very fast rate of travel for East Africa. Stanley dearly
wished to continue this headlong pace. So Stanley promptly
agreed with the overjoyed Arabs that Mirambo was completely
at fault in the quarrel, that he was a cruel, avaricious leader of
bandits, and that progress and civilization in East Africa demanded his immediate downfall. More important, although left

unsaid, Mirambo was blocking Stanley's anticipated route to Ujiji. Thus Stanley joined forces with the Arabs to combat Mirambo, a decision which later caused a chastened Stanley to comment ruefully, "I was tempted in an unlucky moment to promise them my aid." But regrets came later. In August 1871 Stanley, the Arabs, and the Nyamwezi of Unyanyembe were confident of victory as they set off to battle, stirred by the martial sounds of horns and drums and inspired with the blessings of Muslim and African religious men. They can be forgiven this confidence. With their forces numbering 2255 men, 1500 of them bearing firearms and each averaging more than one hundred rounds of ammunition, the Arabs and their allies formed by East African standards a most imposing force.

Mirambo was fully cognizant of the strength of the advancing enemy, preparing to oppose them, according to Stanley's figures, with 1000 armed followers of his own, plus 1500 Ngoni allies. The Urambo *ntemi,* living up to his reputation, had conceived a carefully designed battle plan. His opponents, lacking effective direction since Arab factionalism prevented the selection of any one individual from the ranks of their leaders as commander-in-chief, had not. Mirambo, aware of the Arab irresolution in decision making, consequently cleverly avoided a dangerous direct confrontation with their total force, probably realizing that, once in the heart of conflict, the undoubted bravery of the Arabs in actual battle might have overcome their leadership problems. Therefore, the Unyanyembe forces, meeting little opposition, were able to capture, plunder, and burn Mirambo's village of Zimbizo, plus two other villages, while generally devastating their surrounding countryside. Flushed with this easy success, the individualistic Arab leaders, falling prey to Mirambo's probable intended strategy, began to divide their hitherto united force. Stanley, then bed-ridden because of the onset of a serious attack of fever, later claimed that he strongly argued against the force's division, but if he did so no one paid him any heed. Still confident, over 500 Arab-led men sallied forth to seize the center of Ulyankulu. Mirambo, still awaiting the most propitious opportunity for a decisive strike, remained quiet. Ulyankulu fell to the Arabs without its defenders mounting a significant resistance.

Laden with a rich booty in slaves and ivory from Mirambo's town, the victorious detachment triumphantly began the return march to the main Arab encampment. Their elation was short-lived. Either while carelessly marching along, according to Stanley, or while resting at night without adequate defensive precautions, according to reports received by the French consul in Zanzibar, the Arab forces were ambushed by Mirambo's waiting warriors. All of the Arabs in the group, about twenty, and half of their followers were killed; the shattered survivors, abandoning their booty, fled panic-stricken to the main camp. There the demoralized men mixed with their fellow soldiers, shaking them with the rumor that Mirambo was advancing behind them on the camp. The panic became contagious and the whole allied force degenerated into a leaderless mass, each man hurrying to the supposed safety of Unyanyembe's palisaded settlements. At least one Arab leader, Khamis bin Abdulla, did not lose his self-control; he valiantly attempted to stem the flight, but the panic-striven men were not to be checked by the isolated efforts of this vigorous young Arab. Most of Stanley's men similarly deserted their leader; hampered by his illness he reached safety only after some very harrowing experiences.

Mirambo's careful strategy, which demonstrated the effective control he could exercise over his disciplined followers, had given him a total victory over the largest Arab-led military expedition ever to leave Unyanyembe. That Nyamwezi chiefdom lay open to his advancing army, 3000 men strong. Mirambo had arrived at one of the crucial moments of decision in his life. A decisive victory over the Arabs at the Unyanyembe capital would have sealed his effort to be the master of all Unyamwezi. Even with their military position so quickly deteriorating, the Arab leadership facing Mirambo remained totally incapable of formulating any united strategy for defense. Ignoring the inherent strength of their large numbers of armed followers, most of the Arabs, as well as the Nyamwezi of Unyanyembe, retreated into their strongly fortified residence clusters, their *tembes,* to await individually Mirambo's attack. Stanley did the same, acting in character by hoisting the American flag over his *tembe* and vowing to fight to the end. But to the great surprise and to the unfeigned relief of the anxiously awaiting defenders, no general assault was launched against Unyanyembe. For unknown reasons Mirambo did not undertake a systematic devastation of the scattered Arab and Nyamwezi fortified settlements. He did ravage a considerable part of the spread-out capital—Stanley estimated that about one-fourth of it was destroyed—but the principal *tembes* of the Arab leaders, *ntemi* Mkasiwa, and of Stanley were left alone. The only noteworthy triumph of the Urambo leader came when a false retreat by his warriors led to a foolhardy sally by men commanded by the Arab firebrand, Khamis bin Abdulla. Mirambo's forces immediately surrounded the Arab group; Khamis bin Abdulla and all of his followers lost their lives in the brief skirmish.

With this limited success, Mirambo and his army withdrew, much to the satisfaction of the embattled and demoralized forces of the Arabs. Why did Mirambo leave Unyanyembe when the campaign seemed to be going so completely in his favor? There are two possible reasons advanced by the various biographers of Mirambo. First, that Mirambo had his mind on the world beyond Unyamwezi and that consequently he feared that a total Arab defeat might have unduly antagonized the Arab ruler of Zanzibar, and his British supporters, whom Mirambo wished to win over to his side in his effort to rule the interior trade routes. Second, that Mirambo feared that his men, with any additional victories, would have amassed so much booty that any surviving forces from Unyanyembe could have successfully attacked them on the return to Urambo. The first explanation seems the less convincing. A total victory for Mirambo in Unyanyembe would have left the authorities in Zanzibar with little choice but to deal with the victor, a choice they would not have minded at all if Mirambo had kept commerce moving efficiently. It is also doubtful whether at this early time Mirambo had evolved in his mind a clear conception of the Arab and British position in Zanzibar. He had had very little opportunity to gain extensive information on this distant and very different part of Africa. The second explanation could have some merit, especially considering the unruly nature of Mirambo's Ngoni allies, although it does appear likely that any victory at Unyanyembe would have completely ended any danger of an offensive thrust from the Arab-Nyamwezi armies. A third possibility exists. Perhaps Mirambo simply realized that his army was not equipped to carry out the extended sieges necessary to capture the very strongly fortified *tembes* of Unyanyembe. The longer such a military operation lasted, the scarcer provisions for his troops would have become, and the more likely that a successful Arab sortie might turn the fortunes of war against him. Perhaps a combination of the second hypothesis and the last explanation offered by the author of this work is the best explanation that can be made at the present of Mirambo's conduct. In any case, Mirambo and his booty-laden warriors left Unyanyembe; he never again came so close to defeating his Arab and Nyamwezi rivals for the control of Unyamwezi.

Stanley, who, it is claimed, received a message in his *tembe* in Unyanyembe from Mirambo stating "that he would drive Bwana Stanley back to the coast," was so disgusted with the ineffective Arab performance during the hostilities that he decided he had had enough of the war. Despite the Arabs' earnest pleas that he remain with them, Stanley set off, with a reduced caravan, by a devious route which allowed him to avoid Mirambo's warriors and to accomplish successfully his fateful meeting at Ujiji with Livingstone. Stanley's delay in Unyanyembe in fact allowed him to reach the Lake Tanganyika port town shortly after the Scots missionary-explorer had arrived there. An earlier appearance would have marred his whole venture, since Stanley would have had to cross over into the Congo to find Livingstone without exactly knowing of his whereabouts. In writing of his experiences during the trying period of the hostilities against Mirambo, Stanley, much impressed with the Urambo leader's military abilities even though he then continued to regard him as a bandit leader, christened Mirambo "the African Bonaparte."[1] The appellation has continually been used to describe the Urambo *ntemi,* although some later biographers of Mirambo, notably Roland J. Harvey and John B. Kabeya, have transformed the sobriquet to read "the Napoleon of Central Africa." Stanley's

[1] Henry M. Stanley. *How I Found Livingstone* (London, 1872), 296.

term is fitting enough. Although Mirambo of course operated in a much more limited area than did the French leader, his hold on the imagination of his peoples, and on modern-day Tanzanians, has similarities with Napoleon's lasting place in the European memory.

Whatever the reasons for Mirambo's unexpected withdrawal from Unyanyembe, the war continued with renewed activity on the part of both belligerents. The events of the subsequent campaigns, unfortunately, become more difficult to follow in detail since, with the departure of Stanley, the only European who ever participated in any fashion in the actual fighting, we are without any eye-witness accounts from the armies of either contender. But all available sources do agree that the course of the war now turned against Mirambo. In a surprising turnabout, the Arab-Nyamwezi alliance had somehow overcome its past weaknesses to form themselves temporarily into an effective fighting army. After returning to Urambo from Unyanyembe, Mirambo had regrouped his warriors, leading them once more against the Arabs in September 1871. There was a major encounter at the village of Mfuto, near the Unyanyembe capital, where the Urambo leader suffered a crushing defeat. Information from a Nyamwezi informer, given in the unreliable compilation of F. G. Carnochan and H. C. Adamson, indicates that Mirambo was drunk at the time of the battle, thus providing at least one reason for the Arab victory. If Mirambo's judgment at Mfuto was clouded by *pombe,* his later temperance years may well have been the direct outcome of this loss. Following Mfuto, Mirambo was necessarily compelled to resort to defensive actions to stave off a complete Arab victory. By January 1872 Stanley, while returning from Ujiji to the East African coast via Unyanyembe, recorded a report that the Arab forces were "thundering at the gates" of Mirambo's center of Ulyankulu, their forces buttressed by the timely arrival of reinforcements sent by the Nyamwezi warrior leader Simba (or Kabungando) of Usawila, a brother of the former Unyanyembe *ntemi* Msabila, who had been driven from that chiefdom in a past succession struggle, and by the Nyamwezi of the small but powerful Ugunda chiefdom of *ntemi* Muli-manombe. The inhabitants of Ugunda, protected by some of the strongest fortifications in Unyamwezi, had earlier repulsed Mirambo when he attacked their center; they remained his resolute enemies, ready to contribute their share to Mirambo's downfall. Also probably present in the combined army pursuing Mirambo was a contingent of about 300 armed men hurriedly brought to the fighting by an important Ujiji Arab, Said bin Majid. He came to avenge his son, Soud bin Majid, who had fallen alongside Khamis bin Abdulla during the Unyanyembe hostilities. Hearing all this information so adverse to Mirambo, Stanley felt safe to conclude, with obvious satisfaction, "in a month he will be dead of hunger." If Mirambo's position was really that precarious, it may give credence to the information an Arab passed on to David Livingstone in February 1872 that Mirambo had offered to repay all the goods which his men had taken from the Arabs during their earlier victory. But the Arabs, then very confident in their new position of strength, refused the offer, doubtlessly regarding it as an indication that Mirambo despaired of defeating them in the continuing hostilities.

Fired by the optimism coming from their recent victories, the Arab forces, still nominally led by the *liwali* Said bin Salim, prepared for a major and, it was hoped, final effort against Mirambo during May and June of 1872. Their strength was even further increased when the Arabs trading among the Sangu sent what aid they could to their brethren for the campaign. Even the peaceful Mkasiwa was reported as participating in the expedition. Information gathered by Livingstone told of about 2000 men in the Arab camp poising for an assault on Mirambo's stockade from which Mirambo, not at all disposed to accept defeat passively, had made at least one successful sortie against his enemies. The Arabs even hoped to use their one piece of artillery, a seven pounder of 1679 vintage, to breach the fortifications. Suddenly, however, the entire Arab offensive collapsed. Said bin Salim returned to Unyanyembe, relating to Livingstone that a "general flight" had taken place among his numerous followers, and explaining that this unexpected disaster was due to the hunger of the men. The securing of provisions was of course a consistent problem for large groups of men operating in East Africa, especially in wartime, but Livingstone did not appear to be convinced by the *liwali*'s explanation. The missionary rather emphasized the weak nature of the Arab leadership, an interpretation no doubt strengthened by Livingstone's well-known antipathy to Said bin Salim. He regarded the Arab *liwali* as one of the major slave dealers of east central Africa, a charge denied by Said bin Salim, but one which later observers proved true. Commenting upon the *liwali*'s military leadership, Livingstone claimed that Said bin Salim had left the place of battle before the planned assault to return to Unyanyembe merely for the purpose of carrying on his normal business activities, and implying that this was a common happening among the Arabs since "the success of the war is a minor consideration with all."

With each of the contending parties equally having missed a major opportunity to administer a possibly decisive blow to its rival, the warfare between Mirambo and the Arabs continued without subsequent confrontations of large bodies of fighting men. Mirambo seemingly remained in parlous straits for some time, since July 1873 information received by the British explorer Verney Lovett Cameron as he marched toward Unyanyembe described the Urambo *ntemi* as a harassed fugitive in the bush. But if this were true, the Arabs proved incapable of finishing off their rival, or of even inflicting further major defeats upon his warriors. And as Cameron gained in experience from his stay in the African interior, he learned that Mirambo had, or was regaining, a stronger position than that which he had previously reported. Bands of Mirambo's warriors, fighting effectively through guerrilla tactics, had infested the entire countryside around Unyanyembe, rendering it very hazardous for any Arab supporter to wander far from his *tembe* without a strong escort. Mirambo, meanwhile, had managed to receive adequate supplies of gunpowder from African villages ostensibly allied to the Arabs. They traded their supplies in secret to the fugitive *ntemi,* being joined in this undercover trade by some Arab merchants who refused to accept any direction from the Unyanyembe community. Confirming Mirambo's ability to withstand his enemies, Bishop Steere, whose informants were usually very accurate, reported in October 1873 from Zanzibar that he had learned that the tide of battle had turned against the Arabs. Mirambo, the bishop said, had won an important skirmish by stratagem. Several African leaders, supposedly loyally allied to the Arabs, had turned against them, hitting unexpectedly at their rear and thus aiding Mirambo to victory.[2] Regardless of the accuracy of these several reports, the consequence of the unresolved struggle with Mirambo, marked by the appearance of bands of irregular fighters ranging all throughout Unyamwezi, was that the trade with Zanzibar through Unyanyembe became significantly curtailed. The Unyanyembe Arabs themselves added to the existing commercial malaise by forcibly detaining many passing Arab caravans in their center so that they could impress their manpower for use in the war. The seriousness of the trade blockage to Zanzibar was demonstrated by the rise in the market price of ivory, the Unyanyembe route's main export: during the war years the selling price of ivory doubled.

Thus compelled to pay attention to one of the few inland happenings that could command his interest, the ruler of Zanzibar, Barghash bin Said, who had succeeded his brother Majid in 1870 (he ruled until his death in 1888), turned a worried eye upon the damaging military stalemate in Unyanyembe. The Arab ruler had continuously been besieged with plaintive requests for military and financial aid by his subjects in the interior. For example, letters dated February 1872 received in Zanzibar from the Arab leaders in Unyanyembe described their situation as so dangerous that it imperiled the future of their community. They were, according to British representative John Kirk, "blockaded, unable to trade and short of provisions." Said bin Majid, leader of the Ujiji reinforcements, added that "if any one pass a little outside he is seized and killed."[3] Not everyone accepted the truth of these ominous requests for support, believing them put forward by the interior Arabs as a ruse to utilize the war as an excuse to draw resources from the sultan for their own private

2 Steere to Festing, Oct. 22, 1873, A.1.III, Universities Mission to Central Africa Archives, in Archives of the United Society for the Propagation of the Gospel, London.

3 Kirk to Foreign Office, April 10, 1872, F.O. 84/1357, Public Record Office, London [hereafter PRO]; Said bin Majid to Barghash, February 1872, in *Proceedings of the Royal Geographical Society*, XVI (1871-72), 386.

gain. The fact that several Zanzibar Arabs were fitting out new caravans for Unyanyembe, despite the harrowing stories emanating from its Arab leaders, further belied the letters. And, from our vantage point, the Arabs certainly painted a portrait somewhat different from the scene Livingstone described in his journal at about the same time. Nevertheless, Barghash and his Indian officials, worried by the obvious effects of the war upon the Zanzibar ivory market rather than by any Arab letters, decided to intervene. It was a major policy decision for Barghash, considering the very limited armed forces of the Zanzibar state available for action in inland Africa. But the economic health of his dominions depended upon trade, and without doubt the Unyanyembe Arabs had proved themselves unable to solve the crisis with Mirambo through the utilization of their own military resources. And it was a revolutionary step for a ruler of Zanzibar. Any previous military expeditions sent from the island against recalcitrant Africans had experienced only limited action in areas located fairly near to the Indian Ocean littoral. Barghash was obviously disturbed enough over the effects of the war with Mirambo on the revenues of his dominions to mount the largest and most significant expedition to the distant African interior ever attempted by any ruler of Zanzibar.

The sultan, possessing no trained military hierarchy from which to select a commander, appointed one of his foremost Arab subjects, Amir bin Sultan al Harthi, a long-term resident of Unyanyembe who had returned to the coast early in 1871 after a ten-year stay in Nyamwezi territory, to lead the expedition against Mirambo. Some reports also indicate that Amir bin Sultan was named *liwali* of Unyanyembe in place of the increasingly discredited Said bin Salim. To carry on the campaign, Amir bin Sultan was given command of a reported 1000 Baluchi troops, the mercenary soldiers from the Makran coast who formed the backbone of the Zanzibar army, plus an additional 2000 men drawn from the populations of Zanzibar and the East African coast. It should be noted that the sultan's soldiers had not previously won a reputation as the most reliable of military forces; British representative Henry Churchill in 1868, presenting the common contemporary opinion, contemptuously dismissed them as a "miserable rabble . . . with their antiquated match locks and their shields and their long handed straight swords."[4] Despite its deficiencies, such a large force put a considerable strain upon Barghash's limited exchequer. The Arab ruler was always short of funds, which may explain the "extraordinary request" made by the sultan in June 1873 for a $50,000 loan (for three years at 9 per cent interest) from the American merchant and diplomat, Francis R. Webb.[5] The request was not granted, and the unresolved financial problem had an important effect upon the new measures proposed against Mirambo.

Amir bin Sultan and his army had arrived in Unyanyembe by August 1873. Seemingly forgetting their previous desperate pleas for aid, the leaders of the Unyanyembe Arab community did not welcome the reinforcements dispatched to them at great expense by their sultan. Amir bin Sultan later lamented that "when he reached there, the Arabs did not agree with him, [they] disliked him" and that he was faced by opposition from the unhappy Said bin Salim as well as from the other two leading Arabs, Shaykh bin Nasibu and Abdulla bin Nasibu.[6] The three Arabs obviously looked upon Amir bin Sultan as a potentially dangerous opponent for them in their own squabbles over predominance in Unyanyembe. Even if his expressed mission was to fight Mirambo, they did not consider Mirambo's possible defeat as being worth the cost of their relegation to a secondary position in the affairs of Unyanyembe. An additional measure of rivalry within the Arab ranks might also have originated from the reported departures of many Arabs from Zanzibar after the signing of the 1873 treaty between Barghash and the British further restricting the slave trade. Any new Arab arrivals in Unyanyembe certainly were not trustworthy followers of their sultan, disgruntled as they were by the treaty affecting what they considered as their inherent right to trade in slaves. Thus by December 1873 the Arab rivalry over the direction of affairs had bogged down

4 Churchill to Secretary of State for India, April 14, 1868, Secret Letters Received (Various), 48, India Office Archives, London.

5 F. R. Webb to E. D. Ropes, June 17, 1873, Ropes Papers, Peabody Museum, Salem, Mass.

6 Note in E-67, Zanzibar Archives [hereafter ZA].

the planned new campaign. According to Cameron, the Baluchi forces had thrown in their loyalties to the two Nasibus, while the coastal and Zanzibari men opted for Amir bin Sultan. Said bin Salim apparently did not agree with either of the two Arab groups. Not surprisingly, with these divided counsels, no effective action at all was undertaken against Mirambo.

The continued presence of this large and inactive military expedition in Unyanyembe naturally became a significant drain upon Barghash's treasury. To meet this, in mid-1874, Barghash had to take the very unpopular measure of raising the duty on the ivory coming from the ports opposite Zanzibar, and on cloves coming into Zanzibar from the island of Pemba, hoping thus to secure an additional $100,000 to meet his mounting debts. It should be remarked that this was no pleasurable step for the Zanzibar ruler, who had on his island the reputation—an unfavorable one among Arabs—of being a much more parsimonious sultan than his predecessors Said bin Sultan and Majid bin Said. Thus, disgusted with virtually every aspect of his interior venture, Barghash sent a trusted agent, Abdulla Muhammad, to Unyanyembe to investigate the lack of progress there, and upon confirmation of the obvious discord among his subjects, the sultan in 1875 ordered the return to Zanzibar of Amir bin Sultan and all of his troops. The Unyanyembe Arabs, forgetting their past conduct, protested against the unexpected evacuation, and were curtly informed that if they wished to continue hostilities with Mirambo they could do so entirely upon their own account. According to the lament of the Arabs in Unyanyembe, their sultan had "written to all the people of Unyamwezi saying that . . . Unyamwezi belongs to us and that we belong to it, and that he has nothing to do with the country."[7] All their protests were ignored by the aroused Barghash. When his army returned to Zanzibar, with many gaps in its ranks caused by the ravages of disease, Barghash placed the entire blame for the botched operation upon the two Nasibu brothers and Said bin Salim; he completely exonerated his appointee, Amir bin Sultan. To British

---

[7] Arabs of Unyanyembe to Hashim bin Sualim, 23 Ramadan 1291 in Elton to Foreign Office, Dec. 22, 1874, E-65, ZA.

representative James Elton, Barghash summed all up when he resignedly "declared his inability to do more than had been done, and his fixed determination to leave the Arab colonists to fight their own battles." Barghash was even angry enough at the debacle to speak out against his own long-term interests, asserting heatedly to the consul about Unyanyembe that he "disclaimed all authority over that country."[8]

THE SETTLEMENT

Mirambo had survived another threat. Without knowledge of the exact numbers, or of the psychological state, of his forces at this time, it is impossible to speculate upon what course the Urambo warrior might have followed if Arab disunity had not blocked the utilization of the new men from Zanzibar. According to information given to Cameron in December 1874, Mirambo's followers had been reduced to 150 men, but there is no way to judge the truth of his statement. In any case, by 1875 with the withdrawal of the army led by Amir bin Sultan, at a time when Mirambo appears to have at least in part recovered from his past defeats, the Urambo leader was left in a favorable position in Unyamwezi; conversely the morale of the Arabs of Unyanyembe was at its lowest ebb. Once left to their own resources, the divided Arab community proved unable to organize any forward action against Mirambo. They instead continued to ply Barghash with requests for assistance, but to no avail. Even though this Arab irresolution allowed Mirambo to begin to recoup his fortunes, and to re-emerge as a formidable foe of the Arabs, he had as little wish for a renewal of hostilities as his enemies did. Mirambo now realistically realized that he was unable, for whatever reasons, to defeat decisively the Arabs of Unyanyembe and their Nyamwezi allies. The damaging effects of the gunpowder blockade at the coast imposed by Sultan Barghash against Mirambo certainly contributed to his failure. Mirambo's men could fight without gunpowder, but its absence did leave them at a comparative disadvantage against their rivals. A messenger arriving

8 Elton to Foreign Office, Dec. 22, 1874, Dec. 24, 1874, E-65, ZA.

in Zanzibar in January 1874 had informed British representative
W. F. Prideaux "that as Mirambo is entirely destitute of ammunition nothing is to be feared from him or his adherents."
Prideaux concluded, "in fact, he asserts that there is not a charge
of powder in the whole country."[9] If, when the war began,
Mirambo had been little aware of the influence which Zanzibar
could bring to bear in Unyamwezi, the gunpowder blockade,
plus Amir bin Sultan's arrival in Unyanyembe, had certainly
opened his mind to the necessity of understanding the coastal
world. To demonstrate his new peaceful attitude Mirambo pulled
back his raiding warriors from the Arab trade routes, allowing
the first hesitant Arab and African caravans to pass through his
territories without incident. Some of the traders even moved
safely in sight of Mirambo's own fortified center.

Not content with mere inaction, Mirambo, while apparently
ignoring the Unyanyembe Arabs who could not bring themselves
to admit openly that they could not defeat Mirambo, daringly
dispatched a caravan to Zanzibar carrying a significant amount
of ivory as a formal gift to Barghash. Mirambo announced at the
same time to the sultan that he planned to continue permitting
Arab caravans to traverse his dominions in peace until his delegation returned from Zanzibar. It was a friendly message, with no
threats of punitive actions to follow if Barghash refused to enter-
tain the request for negotiations. The Arab ruler, with the
fiasco of his expedition to Unyanyembe fresh in mind, met this
statesman-like move with a similar action of his own. He was
probably delighted at the inauguration of a contact which could
resolve the unfortunate hindrances to his lagging commerce. But
Barghash proceeded warily so as not to unnecessarily affront his
Arab subjects, many of whose families had suffered personal and
economic loss during the protracted hostilities between Unyanyembe and Urambo. He did not formally accept Mirambo's gift of
ivory, nor did he receive his men. Instead Barghash ordered the
ivory sold and used the proceeds to dispatch to the Urambo
ntemi a return gift of equal value. Since the usual custom in East
African diplomatic encounters was the sending of presents equal

---

[9] Prideaux to Foreign Office, Jan. 12, 1874, E-64, ZA.

in value to those received, Mirambo was left free to interpret Barghash's proceeding as a friendly response. At the same time the wily Barghash could not be accused by any disgruntled Arabs of bowing to their common enemy. After all, no negotiations had ever taken place. Nevertheless the message was clear to all the sultan's subjects; they in addition had already been forewarned by the withdrawal of the sultan's army from Unyanyembe. Barghash had no wish for further hostilities with Mirambo. The Unyanyembe Arabs henceforth recognized that any continuation of hostilities based upon any still lingering hope of eventual aid from Zanzibar was useless. Said bin Salim, long in opposition to additional warfare, and as will be discussed below, possibly already in contact with Mirambo, sent an agent to Urambo in 1875 to conclude peace. The terms are not known, and probably there was no formal treaty; the essential arrangement was that Arab caravans could subsequently travel through Mirambo's territories in peace, with no doubt the payment of the usual passage duties common in East Africa.

Thus the four-year war between Mirambo and the Arabs closed without any apparent advantage to either contending party. Mirambo had gone to war with optimistic hopes of wresting the commercial and political control of Unyamwezi away from the Arabs and Nyamwezi of Unyanyembe. The military success of his previous career against lesser rivals probably made the young leader of warriors confident of defeating any enemy. Mirambo came close to triumph in 1871 at the abortive battle in Unyanyembe, but he did not achieve victory then, and he had few significant offensive successes for the remaining years of the war. With a little more sensible military leadership on the part of his Arab rivals Mirambo might even have been removed as a major leader among the Nyamwezi. Although they had not achieved this result the Arabs and their allies could really be considered the victors since they had essentially maintained their dominating commercial position in Unyamwezi. But they had also suffered heavily from the years of hostilities, particularly on the financial side, because of their interrupted business dealings with the coast. Nonetheless the Arabs remained as openly hostile to Mirambo as they had been during and before the war—even more so. But their leaders, so unsuccessful in battle, had learned a lesson. In the future the Arabs remained content to limit their operations against Mirambo to devious intrigues, leaving any concomitant minor military endeavors to their Nyamwezi or other African allies. Consequently there never was another formal military challenge by Mirambo against the Arab position at Unyanyembe. Another important legacy of the war to the Arab community was that the bitterness caused by their own military ineptitude remained to poison relationships among the Arab leaders. Said bin Salim and the Nasibu brothers had increasingly become enemies, not merely rivals, as the years passed without a victory over Mirambo. When peace came, charges and counter-charges circulated about their respective roles during the war, and especially to their various lines of conduct during the unhappy presence of Sultan Barghash's expedition. It required most of the remainder of the decade of the 1870's to resolve this leadership problem.

Although undeniably suffering a defeat in a major policy objective, Mirambo was not permanently downcast by the turn in his fortunes. The events of the war had introduced this Nyamwezi leader to the distant power of Zanzibar, limited but still present, and to a new factor in his political life, the presence of Europeans. Zanzibar had demonstrated its potential by the dispatch of troops to Unyanyembe, even though they had proved ineffective once there. More important, Barghash had seriously harmed Mirambo's war effort by imposing his effective gunpowder blockade on the coast against Mirambo. Some gunpowder did get through the sultan's inevitably weak administration of the blockade, but on the whole, as noted above, the system proved workable. And even though Barghash accepted the end of hostilities, the gunpowder blockade remained in force. The sultan in 1877 made it a permanent part of his policies regarding inland African rulers. Henceforth all gunpowder was sold by Barghash alone, which besides helping the sultan to gain influence with African leaders, gave Barghash a not unsubstantial profit. Thus if Mirambo wanted to continue expanding his state, even if his moves were no longer outwardly directed against the Unyan-yembe Arabs, he needed at least a passive acquiescence from Zanzibar to allow him the purchase of needed military supplies.

The second new factor, the continuing arrival of Europeans in the East African interior, offered Mirambo the chance to design a new policy to help secure his still desired goal of supremacy in Unyamwezi. Among Europeans only Stanley had fought alongside the Arabs, a proceeding which unknown to Mirambo had brought the American reporter heavy criticism in Europe from many men with African experience. They held such interventions to be an abuse of European power which might prove dangerous to future travelers. In their discussions the concerned European geographers and explorers naturally talked much of Mirambo, however little they really knew of him, thus building upon the more sensational information available from Stanley's dispatches to the *New York Herald,* and in his popular volume *How I Found Livingstone,* to make Mirambo one of the most talked of East Africans in European circles, and therefore naturally a man to be visited by any future expeditions. Without any knowledge of this development, Mirambo had the wisdom to distinguish the abrasive Stanley from other Europeans and to set about attempting to gain allies from their ranks. This required a new line of conduct from the heretofore bellicose Nyamwezi warrior. When Mirambo encountered Stanley once again in 1876, this time in peace—they even became blood brothers—his words as reported by the American correspondent were a fair indication of the policies to come. "But the war is now over," said Mirambo. "The Arabs know what I can do, and Mkasiwa knows it. We will not fight any more, but we will see who can do the best trade, and who is the smartest man." It is an indication of Mirambo's great talents that but for an untoward tragedy he probably would have succeeded in his coming efforts to spread his authority throughout the interior by the effective utilization of the European influence over Zanzibar.

IV

MIRAMBO AND THE EUROPEANS: FIRST CONTACTS

JOHN KIRK AND BRITISH POLICY IN EAST AFRICA

"I OFTEN THINK how much more easily I could rule the country myself instead of bothering with big palavers that too often end in nothing."[1] So said in 1876 the most influential European in East Africa, John Kirk. First coming to Zanzibar in 1866 to serve in a subordinate position on the British consular staff, Kirk, already then possessing more real knowledge of the African interior than any of his predecessors, soon became a valuable, albeit a headstrong, local official. The knowledge had been gained from the four difficult years of working as a member of David Livingstone's Zambesi and Lake Nyasa expedition of 1859-63, giving Kirk ever after, as a former trusted companion of the famous missionary and explorer, a position of great personal prestige in British circles. In 1873 Kirk became the chief British representative in Zanzibar. Thereafter this opinionated, egocentric, and able Scot built himself an impregnable position as Sultan Barghash's adviser, a position ensured irrespective of Barghash's opinions by the overwhelming British predominance in the world of the western Indian Ocean.

The British, drawing upon two foci of authority, from London

---

[1] Kirk to Mackinnon, Feb. 8, 1876, Mackinnon Papers, Box 22, School of Oriental and African Studies, University of London.

and from India, after some early nineteenth-century anti-slave trade activity including the 1822 Moresby treaty concerning Said bin Sultan's East African dominions, had become seriously interested in the region when that enterprising Arab sultan made Zanzibar his chief residence after 1840. Working through a vigorous Indian army officer and diplomatic agent, Atkins Hamerton, the only rival in influence to Kirk among British representatives to independent Zanzibar, the British began to make themselves the indispensable supporters of Zanzibar's Arab rulers. Every concession, however reluctantly granted, to the British in their continuing fight against the slave trade on the part of Said bin Sultan, or his successors Majid and Barghash, further alienated these rulers from their Arab, and even some of their African, subjects. British backing, therefore, became vital for the continuation of the sultans' reigns, lacking as they did the effective military forces often required to keep their recalcitrant followers in check. The sultans had no alternative strengths to draw upon to offset this predominance. Before the 1880's only one other European state, France, had extensive interests in the western Indian Ocean, but the French, faced with the undisputed fact of British seapower, contented themselves with actions in Madagascar and the Comoro Islands. Thus without serious competition from any European rival, Britain by the 1870's, and especially after the 1873 treaty with Barghash ending the sea-borne trade in slaves from the Zanzibar dominions, could normally enforce its will in the Zanzibar ruler's territories. Apart from working against the slave trade, and protecting the resident Indian community, British representatives were not antagonistic to the interests of the Zanzibar state. Rather they generally worked to increase its influence upon the mainland of the African continent, even in the face of the often indifferent attitude of the particular sultan in power, since any extension of Zanzibari influence worked indirectly to further the British, and British Indian, position in East Africa.

John Kirk performed within these broad outlines of British policy. He worked tirelessly in striving to stimulate Sultan Barghash to modernize his state and, once Europeans began arriving in increasing numbers in East Africa, to provide the conditions of security necessary for their missionary, commercial, and other varied endeavors. To Kirk, who completely accepted the normal nineteenth-century European viewpoint of an Africa requiring the stimulations of Livingstone's dictum—commerce, Christianity, and civilization—for its regeneration, his aims for Zanzibar could work only for the good of all concerned, whether Arab, African, Indian, or European. The 1871-75 war between Mirambo and the Arabs, however, demonstrated to Kirk that the accepted policy of working through the Zanzibari ruler and his administrative subordinates, particularly the Indian Customs Master who enjoyed British protection, had severe limitations. Barghash had proved himself virtually incapable of directing events in Unyanyembe, causing Kirk to conclude as early as 1872 that the Nyamwezi chiefdom was "for all practical purposes beyond the Sultan's ordinary jurisdiction." And following the Amir bin Sultan expedition Barghash had simply washed his hands of the affair, thereby confirming his weak position. When the war did end, the initiative was Mirambo's, not that of the sultan. This merely confirmed Kirk's earlier explanation of Barghash's normal authority: "he is not Sultan but feudal chief" over the Arabs of East Africa.[2] Although he never said as much, the Zanzibar policy toward the Unyanyembe-Mirambo hostilities had so fully disillusioned Kirk that he was deterred from taking any additional initiatives designed to extend, through Barghash, the authority of Zanzibar in the distant African interior. Thus British policy, since Kirk's decisions were usually accepted in London, was open to any initiatives, however unexpected, which might come from the man Kirk had previously heard of only as a powerful warrior-leader of a small Nyamwezi state—Mirambo.

THE CATALYST: PHILIPPE BROYON, TRADER

The appearance in the interior of a new type of individual was required to bridge the gap—not in distance, but in way of life—

[2] Kirk to Secertary of State for India, Sept. 2, 1872, Secret Letters Received (Various), 49, India Office Archives; Kirk to Foerign Office, Sept. 7, 1871, in Fitzgerald, Mansfield and Tucker to Secretary of State to India, April 8, 1872, Secret Letters Received from Bombay, first series, 37, India Office Archives.

between Urambo and Zanzibar. The first person to attempt this
task was Philippe Broyon, a heretofore-obscure Swiss seaman
turned trader. Broyon, destined to be one of the most influential
Europeans in Mirambo's life, was born in Bex, Switzerland, in
1844. Seeking adventure, at the age of eighteen he left his quiet
homeland for the busy port of Marseilles, where he shipped on-
board vessels of the merchant firm of Roux de Fraissinet, one of
the principal French commercial houses then active in East
Africa. After several apparently uneventful voyages to Zanzibar,
Broyon, seeking an opportunity to advance his personal fortune,
decided to remain on the island in the employ of the Marseilles
firm's local representative. It was not an unusual decision for an
ambitious young man to make. But after several years' labors,
including a time as the commander of a local Roux de Fraissinet
schooner, Broyon in 1872 decided to abandon his comfortable
life to undertake on his own account a new occupation, that of
a trader venturing into the as yet largely unexplored African
interior. The initial financial backing was advanced by the
French firm's local agent. Selecting a base at the port town of
Sadani, not far to the north of Bagamoyo, Broyon, who was described in 1878 by the unfortunate French explorer, the Abbé
Debaize, as "tall, thin, vigorous, with the carriage of a French
soldier,"[3] immediately proved himself a very capable organizer
of caravans. Once familiar with the complicated local conditions
of commerce, Broyon began leading expeditions inland from
Sadani. He thus earned the dangerous distinction of being the
first European trader to challenge the existing Arab-African
monopoly of the commerce in ivory between the interior and
the coast, a challenge that Arabs like Said bin Salim of Unyanyembe could not long let pass unnoticed, since it was the beginning of a serious threat to their position as middlemen between
the inland Africans and the Indians of Zanzibar. To all who
knew him during this period of his life, especially the experienced
French fathers of the Roman Catholic Holy Ghost mission, the
only European organization then significantly active on the main-

3 Debaize to Mouchez, Oct. 17, 1878, *Bulletin de la Société de Géographie
de Marseille*, 3 (1879), 50.

land, Broyon was a courageous, able, and honest representative of East Africa's small European community, even though, as the mission's superior, Père Horner, reluctantly said, Broyon was a Protestant.

Broyon's first commercial base in the interior was in the area around the small village of Mpwapwa, inhabited by Kaguru and Gogo Africans, but under Gogo predominance; it was a principal supply center on the caravan route to Unyanyembe. Not finding Mpwapwa a very profitable location for his business operations, and suffering from the scarcity of provisions in its difficult environment, the Swiss trader in 1875 began searching for more lucrative places for his commerce, culminating his exploratory ventures with a visit to Mirambo in Urambo. He was the first European to have personal contact with the Nyamwezi ruler. Our information on their relationship is unfortunately severely limited, but Mirambo was obviously pleased to encounter this representative of the outside world. Broyon was fluent in the Swahili language, which Mirambo also knew, and in their conversations Mirambo must have received his first clear synthesis of the political and commercial realities of the East African coast. And of equal importance to Mirambo, Broyon offered the Urambo ruler the opportunity for the profitable transport of his extensive ivory stores to the coastal markets. The success of this ivory trade was very crucial to the development of Mirambo's state. It was the one commodity Mirambo had access to which could regularly gain him the items he and his people wanted from Zanzibar. Mirambo possessed a monopoly on all the ivory originating within his dominions; this was the traditional prerogative of the *ntemi*, as well as of most of the chiefs in east central Africa. He also sent his caravans far and wide in search of ivory; there are reports of Mirambo's men traveling even to Katanga and Manyema, among other distant places, to secure the valued commodity. But Mirambo's previous efforts to achieve a substantial return for his ivory in the Zanzibar market, even before the 1871-75 war with the Arabs, had not pleased him. Broyon's unexpected appearance offered Mirambo a new opportunity for profitable commerce, relieving him from his dependence upon Arab traders, whom he did not trust, or upon his own Nyamwezi subjects, who often fell victim when bartering their valuable wares to their lack of knowledge of the coastal market structure.

Broyon had to be equally pleased with the meeting with Mirambo. He had discovered a strong ruler who, as a trading partner, appeared likely to make his fortune. Thus mutually impressed, the two men became blood brothers before working out the details of their future business arrangements. Broyon also married a woman supplied by Mirambo; he thought, no doubt honestly, that she was a daughter of the *ntemi,* although other later observers revealed that she was really a slave girl not related to Mirambo. Then Broyon returned to Sadani and Zanzibar to conduct the sales of the ivory Mirambo had entrusted to his care and in addition to spread the first direct information, unclouded by the interpretations of his Arab enemies, about the dynamic *ntemi* of Urambo. This enterprising Swiss individual has long been unnecessarily neglected by those interested in East Africa's past since he never returned to Europe to write the customary volume emphasizing his "triumphs" while in Africa. Even the few individuals who then knew of his pioneer work added to this silence, notably Henry Stanley who neglected to mention in his published works that he had met Broyon in 1875 while traveling near Mpwapwa—after all, no one was supposed to anticipate Stanley's travels.[4] Nevertheless, Broyon's return to Zanzibar after his discussions with Mirambo must have caused a considerable stir. The alert John Kirk, who made certain he knew all of especial interest about returning inland caravans, obviously had some valuable information to ponder.

THE BRITISH MISSIONARY INVASION

Unfortunately for Broyon's subsequent career, his exclusive relationship with Mirambo lasted but a brief period. After the very limited European presence during the years before the 1870's, there then occurred a veritable invasion of the East African inte-

---

4 Stanley mentioned Broyon in his journal (which was not published until 1961), but he omitted all reference to him in his 1878 record of his travels. See Richard Stanley and Alan Neame, eds., *The Exploration Diaries of H. M. Stanley* (London, 1961), 28, 119; Henry M. Stanley, *Through the Dark Continent* (New York, 1878), vol. I.

rior by the representatives of various European organizations. Previous to this change the African inhabitants of Unyamwezi and the surrounding regions had experienced only brief encounters with a Burton, Speke, Stanley, Livingstone, or Cameron since these explorers moved as quickly as they could on their way to some distant goal of little interest to Africans. Only Stanley had managed to become involved in local affairs, yet the fiasco of his military experiences was soon over, and in any case Stanley's personal dealings had been limited mostly to the Arab community. The circumstances of the lonely death of David Livingstone ended this period of little contact. Returning to complete his quest in the far interior after being succored by Stanley, Livingstone, traveling with a few African companions, died near Lake Bangweulu, in modern Zambia, in 1873. His followers returned Livingstone's corpse to Zanzibar from whence it went to Britain for a memorable public interment in Westminster Abbey. His death and the subsequent activities it stimulated led to great changes for East Africa. Christian and humanitarian consciences were stirred and money began to flow into depleted missionary society coffers. Badly needed new men came forward, inspired to continue the task of "saving" Africa. While this process continued, additional stimulation for African involvement came from Henry M. Stanley's adventure-filled 1874-77 journey across Africa, from Bagamoyo to the mouth of the Congo River. During this epic trip, often considered the single most important expedition into Africa during the nineteenth century, Stanley visited Mutesa I, the ruler of Buganda. Much taken in by that astute monarch, who wanted Christian support against the Muslim threat to his territories stemming from Egypt's advance southward through the Sudan, Stanley wrote his famous letter of April 14, 1875, to his newspaper employers, the *New York Herald* and *Daily Telegraph*, calling for Christian missionaries to accept the challenge of working in Buganda. Already primed by the events surrounding Livingstone's death, the British missionary societies did not allow the plea of Stanley to remain unanswered for long.

One of the first missionary organizations to seize the challenge was the important Church Missionary Society, active in Africa since the early nineteenth century. A first expedition arrived in East Africa in 1876, led by an efficient former Royal Navy lieutenant, G. Shergold Smith, and including the later famous missionary to Buganda Alexander Mackay. The members of this group, with a planned destination in Buganda or in the neighboring Haya state of Karagwe, did not visit Mirambo on their march through his territories toward their Lake Victoria goal since, justifiably suspicious of Mirambo's war-making reputation, they feared the reception they might receive. The missionaries, though, did send to and receive from Mirambo messages of friendship as they passed through his territory, for which Broyon, then in Urambo, served as translator. And their presence in East Africa was responsible for a decision which led to the arrival of another fateful European visitor to Urambo.

The missionaries required a relief caravan to carry needed additional supplies to their temporary camp on the southern shore of Lake Victoria. Acting in their behalf, Kirk had the Church Missionary Society hire as caravan leader John Morton, a former lay missionary of the British society represented in Zanzibar since 1864, the Universities Mission to Central Africa. Morton had been in East Africa since 1870; personal difficulties had led him to leave the service of his mission and to strike out on his own in 1874. He was a fluent speaker of Swahili, and lacking any other available European to lead the necessary caravan to the waiting Shergold Smith, this talent appears to have decided Kirk on his choice. Morton left from Sadani in March 1877, reaching his Lake Victoria goal in October. Knowing of Mirambo's friendly exchange of messages with the missionaries, Morton stopped briefly to visit Mirambo on his way to the lake. The discussions between the two men were cordial and Morton reported that Mirambo "expressed his friendly feelings for the English, and . . . promised to assist and help forward any white men coming through the interior over which he has control."[5] Mirambo had apparently followed the same course in his meeting with Morton that he had previously done with Broyon. He treated the traveler with open hospitality, opening up to him

[5] Quoted in O'Neill to Wright, Oct. 1877, C. A6/018, CMS.

the possibility of Morton's conducting a lucrative ivory trade in the future on Mirambo's behalf. Morton, without any profitable career open to him in Zanzibar, was ready enough to undertake the new opportunity so suddenly presented to him; Shergold Smith, after talks with Morton, felt certain that he would become "a traveller or resident in the interior."[6] With his job for the mission accomplished, Morton hurried back from Lake Victoria to the coast, carrying an important message to Kirk from Mirambo, to prepare for an independent commercial inland venture. His British nationality, the fact that Kirk had originally hired him to go to Lake Victoria, plus the message he brought from Mirambo, gave Morton greater immediate importance to Kirk than Broyon. He soon was in contact with the British official concerning the importance of what he had learned about the Urambo *ntemi*'s open receptiveness to receiving additional European visitors.

Kirk, still dissatisfied with Barghash's lack of interest in the interior, especially with the increasing arrival of British missionaries for whose safety Kirk bore an important share of the responsibility, decided to utilize Morton on his return to Urambo to open a channel of communication with Mirambo. The once reviled leader of bandits, profiting from his adroit reception of Europeans interested in being on intimate terms with him, had become to Kirk a possible ally for the advancement of British and Zanzibari policy in East Africa. Another reason for Kirk's new policy was the disturbing news of recent events in Unyanyembe which might act adversely upon the safety of British subjects traveling and living in the interior. Said bin Salim, the sultan's *liwali*, had been driven from office by a combination of forces led by Abdulla bin Nasibu and Shaykh bin Nasibu, with the support of the new *ntemi* of Unyanyembe, Isike. Said bin Salim had fled to Mirambo's territory where he had been given refuge at Uyui. Although Kirk was not sorry to see Said bin Salim, the old enemy of Livingstone, removed from his official position—to Kirk he was "a master of cunning and intrigue"— he was little disposed to welcome his locally appointed successor,

Abdulla bin Nasibu. Kirk regarded the new *liwali* as a man of very low character; he complained that "it is incomprehensible to me how the Sultan can tolerate such a man to use his flag and act in his name."[7] Consequently Kirk was not at all optimistic about the future of the Arab community at Unyanyembe and its usefulness in aiding him to keep the interior safe for commerce and for visitors, particularly with Said bin Salim free to intrigue with Mirambo against Abdulla bin Nasibu, Mirambo's determined enemy.

Abdulla bin Nasibu and his colleagues justified their coup by asserting that Said bin Salim had treacherously aided Mirambo all during the recently concluded war, warning him of all impending sorties; Said bin Salim, they said, would report to Mirambo that "we are coming to attack a certain town of yours on a certain day, be ready."[8] Other charges made against the deposed *liwali* included the selling of gunpowder to Mirambo, and the calling for a truce when the Arabs were gaining—so said his rivals—in the war. The charges are difficult to assess. They seem much too similar to the charges the enemies of Musa Mzuri, the pioneer Indian trader in Unyanyembe, advanced during the Arab hostilities against Msabila: that Musa Mzuri was supplying gunpowder to the enemy. There is no hard evidence to prove the charges, which on their face appear unlikely, in either case. Said bin Salim certainly did not cover himself with glory for his conduct of the 1871-75 war, but then neither did any of the other Unyanyembe Arabs. Perhaps Abdulla Muhammad, the agent sent by Sultan Barghash to Unyanyembe to report on the Amir bin Sultan expedition, had the answer. He reported that Said bin Salim had been very aroused by the refusal of any of the Arab leaders to follow his advice; thus he began dealing with Mirambo. But even then any contacts of Said bin Salim with Mirambo would not necessarily have involved treacherous proceedings against his Arab rivals or the Arab cause. Owing his office to the Customs Master of Zanzibar, Said bin Salim would have been most likely concerned with exploring with Mirambo ways in

7 Kirk to Foreign Office, Oct. 15, 1879, Q-22, ZA.

8 Norman R. Bennett, ed., *From Zanzibar to Ujiji. The Journal of Arthur W. Dodgshun, 1877-1879* (Boston, 1969), 101.

which to end the war so that commerce would resume. If Abdulla Muhammad was correct in reporting that Sultan Barghash wished to remove Said bin Salim from office because of his role in the Amir bin Sultan difficulties, but that the Customs Master prevented the sultan from acting, the *liwali* had merely been doing all that he could to protect his master's interests by ending an impossible war. The most likely cause of the coup against the veteran *liwali* was the continuing personal rivalry among the various Arabs of Unyanyembe, based upon quarrels of long standing often stemming from past political or personal differences in Zanzibar. This cause could even have influenced Barghash since, according to Livingstone, Said bin Salim had been a supporter of Majid, against whom Barghash had unsuccessfully plotted during the first years of Majid's accession to their father's position in Zanzibar. But whatever the reason, Said bin Salim had been chased from Unyanyembe, finding a refuge with one of Mirambo's allies, Majembe Gana, the *ntemi* of Uyui. From this convenient refuge, not far from either Urambo or Unyanyembe, Said bin Salim continued to play an important role in the evolving relationships of Mirambo with Europeans.

Thus Kirk, reacting to the divisions within the Arab community of Unyanyembe and to the weak impact of Zanzibar in the interior, decided to take up Mirambo's wishes, as explained in the letters brought by Morton, for a dialogue between Urambo *ntemi* and British representative. It is interesting to note Mirambo's judgment of the power realities of Zanzibar; in the present accompanying the message, said White Father Père Charmetant, Mirambo had sent Kirk ten tusks of ivory while Sultan Barghash received but six.[9] Kirk replied to Mirambo that he had received his message expressing "his desire to open friendly relations and assist in all measures that may lead to increased intercourse and trade in the countries over which he has made himself paramount chief." According to Morton, Mirambo even had offered to advance against the Gogo, in the interests of securing the trade route to Zanzibar, if Kirk so commanded. Kirk

[9] Charmetant's letter of May 16, 1878, in *Les Missions Catholiques*, 10 (1878), 380.

particularly wanted to explore with Mirambo the leading statement that he was "desirous to cement the friendship that exists between the people of the interior and the authorities at the coast and especially to open relations with the British agency and the Government of the Queen of Great Britain."[10] Mirambo was also astute enough to seize upon another tactic besides mere message sending to win over the Zanzibar authorities. Two members of the Church Missionary Society expedition to Lake Victoria had become entangled in a quarrel between a Muslim trader, Sungoro Tarib, and Rukonge of Bukerebe island, located in the southeastern section of the lake. Thomas O'Neill and Shergold Smith perished in the fighting along with Sungoro Tarib. The Arabs of the interior loosely talked of revenge and Mirambo joined in—Barghash had written to ask his aid—by cooly informing Morton that he was anxious to participate in avenging the European and Arab losses. Gerald Hartwig has suggested that Said bin Salim's dealings with Mirambo about this possible action were one reason for his deposition by the Nasibu group.[11]

Kirk therefore considered that all the advances from Mirambo warrented his approaching the Foreign Office concerning what moves should be made to make an ally of this chief, with his strategic location, for the protection of British interests. Kirk noted that he had answered Mirambo's friendly overtures with equally friendly replies, but that this was not enough to satisfy that ruler for long since Mirambo had specifically asked that a European "be sent to help and advise him and offering every assistance in his power to whoever may be sent to teach his people." To Kirk this was a sound proposition; the weak and divided Arabs of Unyanyembe, whose leadership he considered so unsuitable, would be bypassed while a powerful African chieftain would be brought under British influence in a manner that Kirk optimistically hoped might even end the troublesome *hongo* system of the interior. And Kirk thought on beyond any

10 Kirk to Granville, May 3, 1878, F.O.84/1514, PRO; Kirk to Mirambo, July 2, 1878, ZA.

11 Gerald W. Hartwig, "Bukerebe, the Church Missionary Society, and East African Politics, 1877-1878," *African Historical Studies*, 1 (1968), 226-27.

initial discussions with Mirambo. He believed that Sultan
Barghash, acutely realizing his inland impotence following the
Bukerebe affair, could profit from allowing Mirambo to administer the region he had under his influence as a theoretical subordinate acting under the sovereignty of Zanzibar. There would
have been no actual controls from Zanzibar, of course. Mirambo
would act as an independent ruler in his own territories, following the advice he knew came from the British consul, not the
Arab sultan, as long as Zanzibar in return treated him in a
manner giving tangible returns to his state. Then Kirk could
have claimed for Urambo what he claimed in 1884 for the Mount
Kilimanjaro state of Rindi of the Chagga: it is "difficult to look
at Chagga as altogether outside . . . [of Zanzibar] territory seeing
the whole trade is now in the hands of the Sultan's subjects."[12]
The Foreign Office, recognizing that Kirk's plans might work to
the advantage of their usual policy toward Zanzibar, decided to
allow their consul to proceed in his investigations, granting Kirk
general approval for actions which did not commit the British
government to any fixed course.

John Morton, about to return to Urambo to begin his career as
an inland trader, was given messages by both Kirk and Barghash
for Mirambo. The cautious Kirk was still carefully feeling his
way with the distant African chief. His reply to Mirambo of
July 2, 1878, stayed with safe generalities, leaving to the future
any discussions leading to more binding ties between Zanzibar
and Mirambo. The draft of this message shows that Kirk had
initial thoughts of saying to Mirambo, "Now I have to caution
you not to believe all the tales that are brought to you through
the Arabs for they have many intrigues and it is their object to
cause differences between the people of the country." This was
too forward a statement, on reflection, for the accredited agent
to the ruler of the Zanzibar Arabs to make, so Kirk removed it
from his message, perhaps leaving it to Morton to deliver the
words verbally. Kirk was carefully pursuing his plans. When the
Arabs did learn of his dealings with Mirambo they were naturally
aroused. Kirk reported this in October 1878, explaining that the

---

[12] Kirk to Granville, Sept. 27, 1884, F.O.84/1678, PRO.

unhappy Arabs feared the new policy would damage their
monopoly of the ivory trade and that they feared it would end
their own policy of stimulating African leaders to act against
each other so that Arabs might profit from the discord. Kirk
ignored their fears. Mirambo, of course, had little need for Kirk's
advice about dealing with Arabs. He had continued his own
efforts to neutralize the Arabs of Unyanyembe. In February 1878,
C. T. Wilson of the Church Missionary Society had reported that
the Nyamwezi ruler had offered the Unyanyembe Arabs a treaty
containing favorable terms. So at least did Mirambo describe
them. If the Arabs paid a tribute to Mirambo "as a recognition
of his power and status," Mirambo planned to give them the
return of safe and open trade routes through his territory. The
Arabs, not to be swayed from their Unyanyembe alliance, refused
the offer.

Meanwhile Philippe Broyon had been drawn away from his
once-exclusive dealing with Mirambo by the many profitable
opportunities opening to an experienced East African trader by
the continuing numbers of new European arrivals. Another
British missionary group, the London Missionary Society, which
David Livingstone had served in southern Africa for many years,
decided to open a station in the far interior at Ujiji, the town
made famous by the 1871 meeting of Stanley and Livingstone.
A preliminary investigation concerning the route to follow to
Lake Tanganyika was undertaken in 1876 by Roger Price, a
missionary with South African experience. Not recognizing the
widespread presence of the fatal tsetse fly, Price convinced his
superiors that the missionaries could travel inland with ox-drawn
wagons, thus avoiding the many problems always stemming from
the leading of large numbers of Africans in the traditional East
African caravans by inexperienced Europeans. By the time Price
had prepared his expedition, in 1877, he had met Broyon
who also became much interested in the possibilities of the
ox-wagon venture. He helpfully informed Price about Mirambo,
stressing his supposed influence with the *ntemi*, with the result
that the missionary leader requested and received authorization
from London to report on Urambo as a possible site for a London
Missionary Society station.

Price's ox-wagon venture ended in disaster; his oxen died from the disease carried by the tsetse fly, causing Price to abandon his leadership of the mission party, but the rest of the party, now led by J. B. Thomson, another missionary with South African experience, went on with African carriers. Even as they struggled inland, Mirambo recognized their usefulness to his schemes regarding Kirk and Zanzibar. He responded to a Thomson letter requesting oxen for their abandoned wagons by sending instead a group of carriers to aid the Englishmen; he was obviously better informed on the realities of East African travel than were the missionaries. The carriers arrived but they were not used by the missionaries; they appeared too late and they demanded very high wages. Nevertheless Mirambo's goodwill was apparent. And when Thomson's party reached Urambo in July 1878 it received a most hospitable welcome. The fact that Thomson, from his South African years, could speak to Mirambo in the language of the Ngoni no doubt added to the atmosphere of general goodwill.

Mirambo now revealed himself as a first-class dipolmat. Although his contacts with Europeans had been limited to Stanley and the two traders, Broyon and Morton, Mirambo instinctively seemed to know precisely how to act to convince the missionaries of his sincerity, and more important, of his usefulness to their aims. This marked ability to communicate effectively with Europeans of all types remained until the end of his life one of Mirambo's most striking characteristics. After several wide-ranging discussions between Mirambo and his visitors, the lay missionary, Edward C. Hore, one of the better nineteenth-century observers of East Africa, reported: "His acquired power and wealth do not seem to have spoilt the man. He is strictly temperate and actively engaged, as far as I can see, trying to establish a nationality and promote the progress and improvement of his people. He longs for *fundis* (handicraftsmen) to improve his works, and I think entertains a genuine good feeling towards white folks (regarding them, I fancy, just as a people who bring good things into his country)." Hore's colleague Thomson concurred, even though Mirambo had managed to relieve him of his best rifle, and he readily agreed to write to Kirk for Mirambo to help draw the British official closer to the Urambo *ntemi*. According to Thomson Mirambo said: "If the Sultan does not like Said bin Salim to govern Unyanyembe, I will be glad if he will remove Kisessa and put another man in his place. Kisessa is a bad man for both black and white people. Already he has caused much mischief and will cause bloodshed if he is not removed. The Wanyamwezi people have become very bad under him and I will have to defend myself and interests if a better man is not put in his place. Kisessa is making caravans pay hongo and he is very bad. If the Sultan does not like Said bin Salim let him call him to Zanzibar and send another man who will keep the people right and keep the roads open."[13] Thus Mirambo played upon themes he now knew would be welcome in British-dominated Zanzibar, emphasizing the inability of Abdulla bin Nasibu and his followers to make life secure for Europeans. In summary of his conversations Thomson related, "Mirambo says his country is open to all white men, but Kisessa is doing his best to close it." But Thomson and his companions, anxious to reach their Lake Tanganyika goal, were unable to remain in Urambo; they were accompanied on their way as far as the Malagarasi River by men delegated by Mirambo, and consequently the missionaries had to pay little *hongo*. And even before this last kindness the missionaries had been convinced that Mirambo was, in Hore's words, "truly anxious" for European residents and that his efforts to spread his authority could only benefit the European intrusion into eastern Africa by the security such expansion would provide.

These favorable reports, added to the similar accounts of Broyon and Morton, made Urambo a goal of primary interest for most of the missionary societies operating in East Africa. Mirambo was, as portrayed by his admirers, an African personage designed to whet a missionary's appetite. With a strong and intelligent chief, who ruled a large and orderly state, expressing a decided interest in the presence of Christian missionaries, if not yet in Christianity, any missionaries, profiting from his firm authority, would have had a greatly facilitated opportunity to spread their particular creed. The only block to immediate action

13 Thomson to Kirk, Aug. 1, 1878, in Kirk to Mullens, Sept. 12, 1878, Central Africa, 1878-1880, CCWM.

by the London Missionary Society, the first to arrive in Urambo, was their lack of manpower for the task; all of the first expedition was needed for the work on Lake Tanganyika. Thomson, the man on the spot, had recognized the opportunity and the problem facing the London Missionary Society at Urambo even before his arrival at Mirambo's capital. Thus he began discussions with a member of the Church Missionary Society, Dr. E. J. Baxter, who was then heading inland to Mpwapwa. The two men concluded a local agreement, subject to confirmation by their home committees in London, arranging for Baxter to settle with Mirambo, at least temporarily, until the London Missionary Society made a final ruling for or against occupation of Urambo. A probable contributory factor to this hurried decision was the fact of John Morton's earlier visit to Mirambo; on his return to Zanzibar he had recommended to his former society, the Universities Mission to Central Africa, that it move to Urambo. Both the London Missionary Society and the Church Missionary Society men, demonstrating that European political rivalries were not the only elements of discord Europeans would introduce into East Africa, were firm antagonists of the high church doctrines of the Universities Mission, and they wanted to anticipate any decision which the able Bishop Steere might make for his group.

But the London Missionary Society officials in Britain did not approve of the arrangement between Thomson and Baxter. The optimistic reports received from the field had convinced the society's directors that Urambo had too much potential as a successful missionary station for them to risk losing it to another society. Joseph Mullens, the society's Foreign Secretary, called Urambo "the most desirable centre for Christian effort that that portion of the country can present." Thus Thomson was criticized for his agreement with Baxter, and successful negotiations were undertaken with the other interested societies to clear the field of all potential Protestant rivals. Other interested groups, the Roman Catholic White Fathers and the International African Association of Leopold II of Belgium (both to be discussed below), could be forestalled only by a speedy occupation. Urambo was therefore designated for the immediate establishment of a London Missionary Society station.

THE INTERNATIONAL AFRICAN ASSOCIATION

Meantime, Mirambo had a new European arrival from a nation and an organization about which he knew nothing, a group which added major complications to Mirambo's efforts to come to a closer agreement with Kirk. In September 1878 Ernest Cambier of the International African Association arrived in Urambo. Cambier's expedition was the result of an international conference held in Brussels in 1876 presided over by the constitutional monarch of Belgium, Leopold II. The ruler of a small neutral country more interested in its own internal economic progress than in any distant colonial ventures, Leopold nevertheless had dreams, even before his reign began in 1865, of playing a larger role in world affairs than his constitutional status allowed. After a series of abortive schemes for overseas establishments, the tenacious Leopold planned a new initiative. He called the 1876 conference, a meeting including the most famous explorers and geographers of the day, where his skillful management led to the formation of the International African Association, an outwardly private international organization devoted to the creation of scientific and humanitarian outposts in Africa. The international character of the association had a short life, but the organization survived as a largely Belgian group which allowed its president, Leopold, to begin establishing stations in Africa. The initial venture of the association was in East Africa, a region free from European claims of possession, with Lieutenant Cambier leading African carriers inland from Bagamoyo in 1878.

The Belgian lieutenant, inexperienced in African travel, had major problems with his African followers; over 300 had deserted after one particularly troublesome quarrel concerning their wages. But Cambier had persevered in following his orders, reaching Urambo after a difficult passage through Ugogo with the remnants of the expedition. The goals of the International African Association were uncertain then, with the possibility existing that Cambier might establish a station at Urambo designed to function as a necessary support center for later ventures farther inland. Mirambo greeted the Belgian officer with his usual expressions of friendship for Europeans, went through the ceremony of blood brotherhood with his visitor, and quickly promised to recruit from among his own people the necessary carriers required for Cambier's future travels. The two men apparently were able to converse in Arabic. However, according to the report of a later association member, the Nyamwezi leader was somewhat confused over the new arrival's status. Mirambo, said Adolphe Burdo, informed Cambier that there were, to his knowledge, only three kinds of Europeans: the English who always supported him, the Americans who allied with the Arabs against him, and the French, the rest. Undoubtedly Cambier attempted to enlighten his host, but the course of this interesting conversation was not reported. Apart from this minor episode, however, Cambier's stay at Urambo showed Mirambo as a very different man from the genial and attentive *ntemi* heretofore known by his several European visitors.

Mirambo persistently pressed Cambier for gifts, especially firearms, which the Belgian lieutenant very reluctantly gave. This determination to withstand the exactions of Mirambo may explain the subsequent strained relations between the two men. Cambier, an army officer, probably did not act as a missionary or a trader, the only Europeans Mirambo knew; they quietly accepted most of the *ntemi*'s imperious requests with good grace because of the future benefits they hoped to derive from working in cooperation with Mirambo. The Urambo chief, with no knowledge of Leopold's plans for Africa, could have had no other reason for becoming upset over the conduct of his Belgian visitor. Or perhaps Mirambo simply was unable to determine to his satisfaction who this European was, or exactly what organization he represented, and consequently engineered a delay for Cambier until he could fit the visitor, as he had all previous visitors to Urambo, into his plans for expansion in Unyamwezi. Thus Mirambo did not supply the promised carriers to Cambier, continually finding excuses to delay him in Urambo. According to some White Fathers who visited Urambo when Mirambo was absent on a campaign, the only help the African leader actually gave to Cambier was to appoint an official to help the Belgian in his search for men. Since few men were ever found, the official's

task probably was to report concerning Cambier's daily proceedings to his chief. Whatever the explanation, Cambier, made more
unhappy by his own ill health, was soon an enemy of the Urambo
ntemi; his jaundiced reports of conditions in Urambo had a
significant influence upon the next group of Europeans that approached Mirambo's capital.

THE FALL OF PHILIPPE BROYON

Philippe Broyon had at last completed his many preparations
for a return to the interior. But instead of traveling alone, he
was now in the employ of the London Missionary Society, accompanying one of its members, Arthur W. Dodgshun, with a
commission to deliver to Ujiji the supplies the Thomson group
had been unable to carry with them. Along with the missionary
loads Broyon carried goods that he received when he had sold
ivory belonging to Mirambo. Unfortunately for Broyon, however, the other European also engaged in selling Mirambo's
ivory, John Morton, had been unable to return to Urambo with
the proceeds of his sales, and with the messages entrusted him
from Kirk and Barghash. Shortly after leaving the coast Morton
fell victim to a fever so serious that it affected his mental stability. He fatally shot himself while in a fit of depression. His
leaderless caravan suffered some immediate losses of merchandise
from deserting carriers and rapacious Africans of the neighbor-
hood; then it was returned to Zanzibar where Morton's local
creditors secured most of the remaining valuables to satisfy their
claims. Mirambo naturally became increasingly restive over the
whereabouts of the missing return for his ivory; he did not at
all understand the East African credit system, despite Cambier's
well-meaning endeavors to explain the factors affecting Morton's
property. Broyon soon suffered from Mirambo's intense dissatisfaction.

Unaware of Mirambo's unhappiness over what happened to
the compensation for his ivory, Broyon and Dodgshun, who
joined their caravan with an International African Association
expedition under Belgian command which was hurrying to relieve Cambier, marched inland. Then, unexpectedly, came news

of a disaster. A Church Missionary Society party preceding Broyon's group along the main route to Unyamwezi, led by the lay missionary William Penrose, an inexperienced newcomer to East Africa, had been attacked by the warriors of a much feared Nyamwezi raider of the interior, Nyungu ya Mawe, one of the few leaders of that tribe whose military and political skills matched those of Mirambo (Nyungu ya Mawe's career is discussed in Chapter VIII). Penrose was killed in the fighting, while his African followers scattered, abandoning their loads to the raiders. It is now known, from the researches of Aylward Shorter, that the tragedy involving Penrose's caravan resulted from a misunderstanding and that the Broyon-Dodgshun-Belgian group had nothing to fear from Nyungu ya Mawe. But this was not known to the apprehensive Europeans at the time. They instead had to decide how to react to the battle-influenced reports of the many dangers awaiting them if they continued to follow their original route. Broyon, the one experienced member of the combined expedition, had primary responsibility for deciding a course which would ensure the future safety of his party. Initial information reaching the deliberating Europeans mistakenly indicated that Nyungu ya Mawe was an ally of Mirambo, who it was assumed was partly responsible for Penrose's death. Then letters from Cambier arrived, replying to messages sent by the Belgians traveling with Broyon, detailing his unhappy and enforced stay at Mirambo's capital and, above all, implicating Mirambo in the Penrose affair. Cambier, in a very bad mental and physical condition by this period, was acting in all honesty in warning his approaching colleagues, but again the information, based on rumor, was erroneous. The resulting indecision of the Broyon group was resolved by their African carriers; fearing another brush with Nyungu ya Mawe, with or without Mirambo's support, they threatened to desert en masse unless the course of the caravan was altered. It was a reasonable reaction. Broyon was worried enough to be easily persuaded and, in view of the attitude of his African followers, he really had little choice of action. In late January 1879 the caravan then changed direction. It struck out across the little-known territory of the redoubtable Nyaturu peoples, where Broyon had previously traveled. This move was designed to lead the party to Unyanyembe, a place Broyon in 1877 had counseled all European travelers to avoid since he claimed it was a haven of unruly Arabs and slavers, instead of to the original planned goal of Urambo.

The results of his choice were disastrous for Broyon's career as a trader in East Africa; they might have proved equally harmful to Mirambo's efforts to win British friendship. The Swiss trader and his companions passed swiftly and safely as far as Uyui, the refuge of the exiled Said bin Salim, whom Dodgshun described after their first meetings as "a bland, kind old gentleman, apparently quite frank and artless." There the Europeans had to stop when their carriers deserted—stimulated, it was claimed, by the former *liwali* of Unyanyembe, not quite the man that Dodgshun had described, who was now allied to Mirambo. That Arab also wrote to inform his African protector of the Broyon group's arrival. Since it had proved impossible to secure new men in Uyui without Mirambo's support, Broyon hurried off to Unyanyembe in search of reinforcements. There was no thought among any of the confused Europeans of going to Urambo to attempt to put matters in order, Dodgshun later explained, since they had learned that Cambier had been "practically kept prisoner there." Mirambo's supposed attachment to Nyungu ya Mawe also influenced their proceedings. Broyon did succeed in recruiting some carriers with the aid of the Nasibu brothers in Unyanyembe, but all his efforts ended in disaster when Mirambo, fully informed of Broyon's movements by Said bin Salim, sent warriors to Uyui to seize all the loads of the Broyon-Dodgshun caravan, obviously acting to ensure possession of what he considered were the goods Broyon had received at the coast in return for Mirambo's ivory. Cambier, meantime, had at last left Urambo for Uyui. There was one dangerous episode relating to him during the Uyui seizures. Thinking that the Belgian goods were also to be taken, the worried officer prepared to blow them up, but Mirambo's men left Cambier and his relief caravan alone. Mirambo probably did not have any plans to take the loads of the International African Association, but the tense Uyui situation had certainly justified Cambier's fears. His ex-

treme actions, however, permanently left a tarnish on his reputation among those in East Africa who spoke English; they
considered that he had lost his head unnecessarily over Mirambo's conduct. Cambier defended his actions, claiming he had to
leave Urambo quickly because Mirambo had threatened his
safety, but Mirambo denied the charge and most Europeans believed the African leader's version of the affair. Following the
seizure of the loads, all of the Europeans proceeded to the safety
offered by the Arabs at Unyanyembe, there to await the resolution of the crisis.

Mirambo had posed an unwanted problem for the various
European groups, governmental and missionary, trying to utilize
him in their efforts to create stability in the East African interior.
Was the Urambo *ntemi* returning to his supposed bandit past,
thus proving himself unsafe for European associations? However,
apart from the men of the International African Association,
most of the Europeans involved were too committed to interaction with Mirambo to face the alternatives which inescapably
followed from an establishment of his guilt. Thus a scapegoat
had to be found, and since John Morton was dead, the obvious
candidate was Philippe Broyon. This Swiss national, an independent trader lacking a real connection to either the British
government or a British missionary society (even though Broyon
had asked for and received British protection in 1877 from Kirk
who thought he might prove useful to British interests), was to
be sacrificed, paying heavily for what certainly was an honest
error of judgment.

From the British point of view there was at least a prima facie
case to make against Broyon. The Swiss trader had been com-
missioned to sell Mirambo's ivory, to purchase goods with the
proceeds, and to take them to Urambo. Since Mirambo claimed
that he had been cheated by Broyon, Kirk felt that the African
leader had adequate reasons for seizing the loads Broyon carried.
How was he to know which of the many bales of Broyon's
caravan belonged to the London Missionary Society? This interpretation received positive support from Mirambo when he
wrote, not long after the Uyui seizure, to Arthur Dodgshun in
Unyanyembe that he was free to visit Urambo in safety to claim

the property belonging to his society. That Dodgshun had feared to entrust himself to Mirambo and instead had hurried on to Ujiji where lósses in the original mission party made his presence essential, was a regrettable, but understandable, decision. Thus, almost all observers concluded, the fault lay with Broyon and not with Mirambo, and there needed to be no interruption of Mirambo's relations with Europeans. Practically the only words favorable to Broyon came from his missionary companion, Arthur Dodgshun. When they began the trip inland Dodgshun said of the trader to his directors: "You may have every confidence in Mr. Broyon both as to honesty and ability." After the expedition had suffered the exactions of Mirambo, Dodgshun had not changed his mind; before he left for Ujiji he clearly affirmed that Broyon had done everything possible to safeguard the London Missionary Society possessions. No one paid Dodgshun much heed, however.

Broyon was aghast at this turn of events. He at once attempted to clear his name with John Kirk, the most important individual for his continued career since Kirk's decision would necessarily be accepted by all British subjects concerned. Broyon made some very telling points in explaining his relationship with Mirambo. When he began his commercial alliance with Mirambo in 1875, the Swiss trader informed Kirk, he had found that Mirambo made impossible demands for the returns he wished to receive for the sale of his ivory, demands no doubt coming from his genuine unfamiliarity with the East African market. This disenchantment with Mirambo can be dated by third-party evidence as coming before Broyon's troubles at Uyui. In 1878 Broyon had informed the Abbé Debaize that Mirambo, really—he now confessed—only the ruler of a very small state, had an overrated reputation in Europe and that he was a cruel tyrant whose whim was law. Broyon was probably thinking of his own experiences when he told the French priest that even if Mirambo did not require Europeans to pay *hongo,* he received its equivalent by concluding blood brotherhood with his visitors and then demanding as due him as a brother what would have been the *hongo.* Continuing in his explanations to Kirk, Broyon reported that when he demurred at the demands from Mirambo which he

held unreasonable, the Nyamwezi chief simply cut him off from
receiving the necessary carriers for returning to the coast until
the stranded trader caved in. On arriving at Zanzibar in February
1877 Broyon asserted he had sold Mirambo's ivory for the best
return possible. Shortly afterwards Mirambo sent down additional lots of ivory for sale, but this time Broyon, already wary
of additional dealings for the demanding Nyamwezi leader, refused to handle them, directing Mirambo's men to Indian merchants instead. As might be expected, the men did not get the
return Mirambo desired; they received even less than they would
have if they had dealt with Broyon. Broyon by then considered
their dealings no concern of his. He also retained the loads he
had previously collected for Mirambo, fearing that without his
guidance Mirambo's carriers might lose them on the way back to
Urambo. Broyon's unsuccessful attempt to emulate the London
Missionary Society ox-wagon venture, and the proceedings involved in organizing a caravan for that society, added even longer
delays in the return of the loads to Mirambo. Nevertheless, when
he did set off with Dodgshun, Broyon claimed that he carried
all that he owed to Mirambo, with plans to forward the loads
to Urambo when his diverted expedition halted in Uyui.

At Uyui—Broyon bitterly went on—the real villain was Said
bin Salim; he had been a determined enemy of the Swiss trader
since Broyon had attempted to break the Arab-African monopoly
in the Arab trade by going inland. Another fact Broyon did not
add was that the Arabs in general probably had no love for him
since he and Alexander Mackay of the Church Missionary Society
had pursued an Arab slave caravan near Sadani in 1877 and
Broyon had fired at and wounded one of the caravan members.
Then, Broyon continued, the former *liwali*—who needed to
curry favor with his protector since he might some day restore
him to his lost position—by exaggerated reports of Broyon's
proceeding directly to the Unyanyembe Arabs, stimulated Mirambo to act. And Broyon in his account rejected Mirambo's
allegations about his delayed loads. He said, "the true reason . . .
appears to me to be that in consequence of my choosing to take
a different route, he had lost an opportunity of extorting valuable presents from me, as he did from Mr. Cambier, and being

sorry for it he tried to make up his loss by plunder." Finally, Broyon concluded, Mirambo was making impossible demands over what he claimed was still owed to him, and he threatened Broyon with death, with the same penalty for anyone who traveled with him, if he attempted to journey anywhere in Mirambo's sphere of influence. The message was clear enough: Broyon threw himself upon Kirk's mercy. Without a favorable decision his career in inland Africa was ended.

John Kirk, sifting all of this information in Zanzibar, had no doubts about who was at fault. He considered Mirambo "fully justified" in the seizure of the loads since he had been "grossly ill-used if not cheated by Broyon," and that if Dodgshun had not been "scared off" from collecting his society's possessions by the exaggerated accounts of Broyon and Cambier, all would have passed without trouble to British interests. As it was, thought Kirk, the whole matter was a "disgraceful muddle." And Broyon was the one at fault. Relying largely on the testimony of a trusted African, Juma Nasibu (he had once served the explorer Cameron and had then entered into the service of the London Missionary Society), Kirk decided that Broyon had managed "to make as much mischief as possible and by spreading false reports to make both Mr. Dodgshun and the Belgians afraid to venture near Mirambo." The cause of all this trouble, Kirk asserted, was the loads Broyon had not delivered to Mirambo; therefore Mirambo had good reasons for his seizure of Broyon's caravan. Kirk might have remembered his 1871 reactions to the desires of Mutesa I of Buganda when he sent ivory to Zanzibar, responding to an 1868 expedition of Sultan Majid to Buganda, in an effort to further stimulate trade relations between the two countries; Kirk had lamented that Mutesa demanded "very considerable returns for what he has sent down."[14] The similarities in the unreasonable wishes of the two African monarchs were apparently lost on the aroused British official. And in the coarsest nineteenth-century racism, Kirk concluded, in reference to Broyon's African wife and family, what else could one expect from a man traveling with a "native establishment of women and half-caste children"?

14 Kirk to Bombay Government, Nov. 13, 1871, E-61, ZA.

As for Cambier's difficulties in Urambo which had influenced the Broyon group's decision to avoid Mirambo, Kirk simply shrugged them off, harshly reporting that Cambier had gone "rushing off in a fright at Mirambo who laughs at him. Other men go to Mirambo and find him an honest fellow but he must be met by a man."

There the matter rested, despite additional pleading from Broyon when he was able to return to Zanzibar after abandoning as unfeasible his original plans to proceed to Lake Tanganyika, where he hoped a period of elephant hunting would allow him to recoup the losses of his seized caravan. In view of the slurs on Cambier's character that were circulating at the time, it is only just to record that he accompanied Broyon back through Mirambo's territory, despite the Urambo chief's threats, before setting off on the business of the International African Association. With Mirambo opposing Broyon's inland travel there was little hope of his attracting men to serve under his direction, or of commissions from interested Europeans. And Kirk's devastating opinions were known to all. Broyon ultimately settled on the banks of the Kingani River, about fifty miles from Bagamoyo, to attempt growing tobacco. He died there in 1884, perhaps poisoned by his African neighbors in revenge for some local quarrel, leaving an estate insufficient to pay his creditors. Thus ended obscurely the career of Mirambo's first European acquaintance, a man who had early styled himself Philippe Broyon-Mirambo, because of his marriage to Mirambo's supposed daughter, and who had hoped thereby to become one of East Africa's most successful traders. Despite his failure Broyon deserves an important place in the history of European expansion into East Africa. He was the first European to challenge the Arab-African monopoly of carrying ivory to the coast, braving the dangers that his lightly armed caravans had to face from Arab intrigues. The later European arrivals, especially the missionaries, profited in organizing their caravans from the advice that only he could give about the interior. If he had been of British nationality, Broyon might have received the understanding which would have allowed him to recover his standing with Mirambo, and thus to rebuild his career. But he was not and his life as a trader ended, although his example was not lost on the later European individuals who similarly challenged the Arab-African ivory monopoly.

Kirk meanwhile had acted promptly to attempt to bring Mirambo back to his usual friendly disposition toward European visitors. Messengers carried presents from Kirk and the Sultan of Zanzibar to Urambo worth more than the presents Mirambo had earlier sent down. The results of this mission, as reported to Kirk, were satisfactory, and never one to deny himself any credit, he informed his superiors that "I now know that the timely arrival of my messengers and letters probably averted a war with the Arabs of Unyanyembe, and saved the members of the Belgian Expedition and others, by causing Mirambo to distinguish between Europeans and not judge us all as he had Monsr. Philip Broyon and the late Mr. Morton."[15] Kirk's assertions probably were not true, although he believed them; they did at least make good reading in London. Mirambo had sent one of his relatives carrying ivory to trade along with his answer to Kirk. Kirk readily agreed to help arrange the terms of trade, returning the relative to Urambo with more correspondence for his chief. The British official's main fear for the future was the Abdulla bin Nasibu-Said bin Salim rivalry, so Kirk added a letter to the deposed *liwali* offering to guarantee his personal security and freedom from arrest if he returned to Zanzibar. For Kirk, the Broyon affair was closed and he had to get on with the important business of his interrupted negotiations with Mirambo.

15 Kirk to F.O., May 31, 1879, Q-22, ZA.

V

MIRAMBO AND SOUTHON

THE LONDON MISSIONARY SOCIETY directors not unnaturally agreed
with Kirk's resolution of the Broyon affair, adding their own
opinion that the Sultan of Zanzibar was not doing all that he
should to keep the Arabs of Unyanyembe and others in the interior in order. "Can he not," inquired Foreign Secretary Joseph
Mullens, "put a stop to their quarrels with Mirambo and other
native chiefs and bring the delinquents down to the coast to be
judged as they deserve?"[1] Kirk must have smiled at this query;
the obvious inability of the sultan was the prime reason for his
policy of negotiating with Mirambo. The society still wished to
continue with its former plans for a station at Urambo, despite
the recent difficulties, a move encouraged by Kirk's opinion of
Mirambo's innocence. But with the society's ranks badly depleted by losses in Ujiji, where both Thomson and Dodgshun
had died before being able to accomplish any significant work,
an advance toward Urambo required additional reinforcements
from Britain. And in view of all the confusion resulting from
the London Missionary Society loads which Mirambo still held
at his capital, Joseph Mullens himself resolved to take the extraordinary step of proceeding to Zanzibar for the purpose of
gathering all relevant information concerning Mirambo, and

---

[1] Mullens to Kirk, April 4, 1879, unindexed volume, ZA.

then possibly to lead the new mission party inland if it was decided that Urambo was a safe place for a London Missionary
Society station. But the issue was prejudged enough toward a
decision in Mirambo's favor that Mullens and his associates left
London bearing gifts for the Urambo *ntemi*.

Mullens was quickly convinced in Zanzibar. There still remained some worry about Mirambo's attitude to the missionaries; Edward Hore, for example, had written in April 1878 that
Mirambo was very dissatisfied with all Europeans because of the
losses he attributed to Broyon. Nevertheless Kirk had known
since at least as early as May 1879 that Mirambo had affirmed
that he was willing to return the London Missionary Society
loads. Mullens decided that Mirambo should be visited. But
Mullens, an older man who never should have undertaken the
rigorous journey inland, died before his expedition reached
Urambo. The others of the party continued onward with the
full expectation of a friendly reception from Mirambo; he had,
upon hearing of their advance, sent presents of oxen to demonstrate that there was no danger for them in visiting Urambo.

Included in this London Missionary Society expedition was
Dr. Ebenezer J. Southon, a medical missionary, who became the
most important European personal influence upon Mirambo's
life. Southon's detailed letters and journals of his experiences

Dr. Ebenezer J. Southon,
in the 1880's

with Mirambo remain the basic source materials for any account of the Nyamwezi leader's career. Before his arrival in East Africa, Southon had led an extremely varied life. Born in Gosport, Hampshire, in 1850, Southon had followed the usual course of schooling until the age of fourteen; he then pursued "a thorough business education" until he was nineteen. Next came two years of service with a homeopathic physician in London, one year as a dispenser and the next as an assistant. Southon then emigrated to North America; he spent from 1871 to 1874 in Texas. There, probably on the strength of his British medical experience, Southon gained the title of M.D. (he always thereafter carefully listed himself as M.D.U.S.A.) and practiced medicine for two years on the frontier. He also later wrote that his American experience included a period as editor and part-owner of a weekly New York newspaper. Men who talked with him in East Africa reported that Southon while in Texas had been a surgeon in the United States Army. John Kirk, when angry later over the Carter and Cadenhead affair (discussed in Chapter VI), even asserted that Southon was a naturalized American citizen. Returning to Britain, Southon in 1877 applied for admission to the ranks of the London Missionary Society, describing his occupation then as a successful "Commercial Traveller and Commission Agent." The society rejected his application; their reasons were his age and his dependent mother. But Southon, manifesting the determination he later practiced in Africa, persisted, asking to meet the deciding committee in person. After hearing Southon, the missionary board reversed the decision. Southon was sent for more medical education to the Edinburgh Medical Missionary Society; the London Missionary Society allowed him two years of training, rejecting Southon's later plea for a four-year course so that he could qualify for the British M.D.

Southon's pastor's evaluation of him for the society in 1877 was a just description of the man: he "is possessed of a healthy frame. He has knocked about the world a good deal, having been in Texas and other parts of America, has a very fair knowledge of surgery, much mechanical skill, and a fund of common sense. . . . His education has not been as good as I could wish (or he either) but I believe he has a taste and capacity for languages, furthermore he can rough it." In short, Mirambo, who had been anxiously waiting for a European resident, was finally to receive an individual who was well prepared for the difficult task of living with the Nyamwezi leader in Urambo and who was as well trained through past experience as any European then in the interior to serve as Mirambo's contact point with the outside world. It was an important, responsible position; when Mirambo henceforth wrote to Zanzibar his words would appear ás Southon interpreted them. Mullens had given Southon an important role in his ill-fated caravan, and the medical missionary marched inland with an exultation which he said "made me sing for joy and shout with gladness," transposing an American marching song for his African carriers:

> Hurrah! Hurrah! sound the jubilee
> Hurrah! Hurrah! we're marching from the sea
> And so we sing the chorus from Sâadani to the lake
> Whilst we go marching to Ujiji.[2]

Southon arrived in Urambo in August 1879; he and his colleagues received Mirambo's usual hospitable welcome for missionaries, including a ceremony of blood brotherhood between Southon and Mirambo. Southon left a very brief account of the ceremony; Thomson's August 1878 description of the same event is more complete:

> The chief took us into a private house. He had two men and I had my two head men. He uncovered part of his stomach and I did the same. One of my men took the knife and made the slightest incision so as to draw one drop of blood, one inch to the left and one inch and a half below the navel. One of his men did the same to me. My man put a little butter on a green leaf and put the drop of blood from the king on the butter. The chief's man did the same with the drop of blood from me. Then the two men exchanged bloods and my man gave the leaf with my blood on it to the chief and he rubed [sic] it into the cut on his stomach and I did the same with the other. Then the king tore his leaf over my head and I tore mine over his head and thus ended the ceremony and we were pronounced blood brothers.[3]

2 Southon's Journal, June 15-July 11, 1879, Journals: Central Africa, 1878-1880, CCWM.

3 Thomson to Mullens, Aug. 4, 1878, Central Africa, 1876-1878, CCWM

Despite the ceremony and the welcome, the newcomer to Africa was somewhat nonplussed by the warrior chief of whom he had heard so many conflicting stories. Southon graphically reported: "My first impressions of Mirambo were decidedly of an unpleasant nature. He appeared as simply a bandit chief and as he stood surrounded by his fierce looking men, clad for the most part in stolen goods [taken from the London Missionary Society's loads!], and all excited as of with wine I did not have so great a respect for him as I had hoped I should. His face showed a careless *abandon* and his frequent jokes to his excited followers told I thought of either a suppressed anxiety or exultation." But despite the emotional experiences of the first meetings with the famous war leader, Southon had a perceptive eye for other less dramatic, but more revealing, aspects of Mirambo's character. He was prepared to disagree with his colleague, Hore, who had said that Mirambo had demonstrated a "child like waywardness and surprize [*sic*] in the presence of white men." Rather, Southon countered, "his curiosity, I think, is not simple wonderment, but an intelligent desire to know and understand things. He handles a new thing as thoughtfully as a skilled mechanic would a piece of beautiful mechanism, the working of which he does not yet understand." Nevertheless, Southon concluded, "there is a large mixture of 'don't care' about him and a reckless look which tells of a life of continuous daring and ever changing fortune."

In all, with these varying impressions, Southon was captivated by the new personality before him, and he was ready to undertake a residence at Urambo with enthusiasm. He had seen no other African center rivaling the size of Ikonongo, Mirambo's new village. Within it, Mirambo's own residence, built in the style of the East African coast, was surrounded by walls twenty-two feet high and four feet thick. Grouped around the royal living area were about 200 huts, "well built and some of them fifty feet in diameter"; there were many more huts clustered around the outside walls. Many smaller villages were located not too far from the larger center. Southon estimated the population to be 10,000. Whatever the accuracy of his judgment, the number was certainly an impressive one for his missionary labors.

SOUTHON, BRITISH "AGENT" IN URAMBO

Mirambo must have recognized Southon's open attraction to him. He was already experienced enough in meeting and discoursing with Europeans to have precise ideas of his visitors' interests and wishes. And here at last was his long-awaited opportunity to gain the British resident he had so impatiently sought. Mirambo had absolutely no interest in the tenets of European Christianity; furthermore he was honest enough never to really mislead a single European missionary into thinking that he had any serious thoughts of becoming a Christian. He had also, according to a later companion of Southon, Walter Hutley, refused to respond to Arab attempts to convert him to Islam. The basis of Mirambo's interest in the continued presence of Southon must have seemed distressingly clear when in December 1879 he told the missionary that he wanted men "to teach the people how to make guns and powder and cloth." Increasingly, Mirambo was beginning to realize that European knowledge, which was mastering the environment of the nineteenth-century world, could prove a great boon to the welfare of his state and people. Thus if new European arrivals, who in their limited numbers never appeared as a threat to Mirambo's political position, were prepared to impart their knowledge in return for the price of talking about their alien religion, they were welcome to do so in most instances without any interference at all from the African leader. Fortunately for Mirambo and his interests, he had present in Southon a man never content to busy himself exclusively with matters spiritual; his was a practical Christianity, designed more to influence Africans by good works, especially those resulting from his medical skills, rather than by extensive bouts of preaching. This was also a practical decision for Southon since he, along with all contemporary Europeans, had no previous knowledge of the Nyamwezi language. It was one of the major tasks awaiting Southon to master this unknown tongue so that he and his successors could effectively enter into meaningful contact with the Africans living in and around Urambo. In the meantime, while Southon developed his own characteristic approach to missionary work, the two lively intellects of Mirambo and Southon remained in constant play and replay during their years in Urambo. The result was one of the firmest friendships, based on mutual respect for each other's integrity, that ever flourished between an African ruler and a European missionary.

Mirambo immediately attempted to utilize the missionary in his continuing effort to establish a significant relationship with John Kirk. Mirambo directed Southon to write to Kirk in order to determine why no adequate response had come following the letters sent to Zanzibar via John Morton. Apparently there had been additional letters, for the puzzled Mirambo complained, "I send him [Kirk] about one thing and he writes about something different. Perhaps the Arabs [often used as scribes when no Europeans were available] don't write what I tell them." But now using a reliable intermediary, Mirambo listed his desires. First there was the matter of his intensive dislike for the *liwali* in Unyanyembe. Mirambo said,

I want Kissesa removed from Unyanyembe. He takes big mhongo from all caravans, sometimes two hundred cloths from one. If the Wasukuma go to buy oxen, Kissesa takes one doti amerikani [a measurement of the popular cloth produced in New England] for every ox they buy. One caravan he made pay him 200 mapembe [hoes] before they could buy a single ox. Caravans with ivory can only exchange at the rate of one frasilah [about thirty-five pounds] for two pieces amerikani. The Sultan of Uvinza says he makes big mhongo at the Malagarazi [River] because Kissesa makes big mhongo for him at Unyanyembe. Kissesa sent to Mtesa to get men to fight me and nine thousand men started to come, but there was not enough water on the road for so many, so they went back. Why does he do these things? I don't want to fight, but I am quite ready to do so and all my people want me to. They say, "Mwami [chief], take us to fight Kissesa, he very bad man." What can I do? If I don't fight Kissesa, he will fight me. You tell Dr. Kirk if Kissesa is not removed before the end of the Masika [the rainy season] I will lead my people to fight, and tell him that I won't be responsible for any caravans being attacked, the road will be closed and if white men or Arabs get killed don't blame me. Tell him Nyungu [ya Mawe] will help me and he knows that if Nyungu's people go to fight, no one can get to Unyanyembe or Uyui, because the road will be closed. If Dr. Kirk doesn't want my people and caravans to come to Zanzibar all right, let him say so, I don't care. Tell him this is the last letter I will write to him unless his answer be a good one. Ask him why his letter to

Said bin Salim was sent to Kissesa instead of straight to me? I took
S. B. S. out of the pori [bush] and fed and clothed him ever since he
was turned out of Unyanyembe, and he has no cloth of his own to
travel with and I don't intend to give him any.[4]

Clearly Mirambo, with this list of complaints, was undiplo-
matically annoyed at his lack of progress with Kirk, and he was
ready to say so openly in an effort to shake the hesitating British
official into actions meeting his demands. Southon attempted to
moderate the Urambo *ntemi*'s wrath by suggesting that he allow
Said bin Salim to return to Zanzibar to explain in person the
whole unpleasant Unyanyembe situation. Perhaps Kirk in Zanzibar had prompted Southon to this request by informing him
that the removal of Said bin Salim from Mirambo's protection,
which Kirk had failed to achieve, might prove a good start in
quieting Unyamwezi by ending the intrigues between Abdulla
bin Nasibu and Mirambo concerning the fate of the deposed
Arab representative. Mirambo, unwilling to lose a hostage potentially of use to his schemes, peremptorily refused the suggestion, maintaining that this step was impossible since any
movement of Said bin Salim to Zanzibar could be accomplished
successfully only by the aid of a large armed escort because
Abdulla bin Nasibu had vowed to kill him. Mirambo confessed,
to Southon's quiet disbelief, that he lacked the warriors needed
for such a journey. More to the point, Mirambo added, "I want
him [Said bin Salim] to be Governor of Unyanyembe, for he is
a good man and wants to live in peace with everyone." Southon
had to rest content with informing Kirk that Mirambo had told
him all of the above message in calmness and in determination.
Obviously, even though Southon did not openly suggest it to his
touchy official correspondent, Kirk had better take immediate
notice of Mirambo's forcefully expressed wishes.

Despite the lengthy barrage of complaints, Kirk continued the
policy he had been pursuing since his first communications with
Mirambo. He perhaps expressed this policy best, with a typical
nineteenth-century British empire style, in a letter of December
7, 1878, to J. B. Thomson of the London Missionary Society. "I

[4] Southon to Kirk, Sept. 9, 1879, K-1, ZA.

have always held," Kirk postulated, "that the true way of ele-
vating Africa is by raising the standard of the native rulers and
for this purpose I am backing Mirambo for he has power certainly and is quite willing to be influenced." The confident Kirk
doubtless reasoned that what he had accomplished with the initially reluctant Barghash bin Said of Zanzibar could also be done
with Mirambo of the Nyamwezi. But Kirk, despite all the appeal
Mirambo had to those working to advance British interests in
East Africa, doubtless felt compelled to agree with Edward Hore
who, although sympathetic to efforts at working with Mirambo,
characterized him in April 1879 as "a thorough savage."[5] Thus
Kirk's policy had to be shaped accordingly, particularly since his
superiors at the Foreign Office were consistently very wary about
entering into any binding arrangements with African rulers. As
Lord Salisbury said at about this time concerning some proposed
increased dealings with Mutesa of Buganda, "unnecessary relations on the part of our Govt. with pure barbarians seldom end
well," buttressing his position with a reference to the difficulties
of the 1860's with Tewodoros, the ruler of Ethiopia—difficulties
which had required a costly expeditionary force to be sent into
Ethiopia to rescue imprisoned British subjects. Therefore Mirambo's complaints, however forcefully expressed, brought no
change in Kirk's evolving policy; he would use Mirambo as much
as possible to stabilize his part of the African interior, but Mirambo had to remain satisfied with a missionary instead of an
official European resident. No more formal alliance was possible.
  Mirambo had no recourse except to be, if not content, at least
resigned to working within this framework, withal continuously
striving to achieve more positive results. As for the problem of
Abdulla bin Nasibu, there was little Kirk could do to please
Mirambo since the Sultan of Zanzibar did not then think that
he possessed the power necessary to remove his subordinate. As
early as 1871 Kirk had complained that Unyanyembe had "for
some time been led by a set of avaricious unprincipled men whose
acts of extortion both on natives and the poorer Arabs have for
some time back been complained of to . . . Barghash who is im-

5 Hore to Mullens, April 16, 1879, Central Africa, 1879, CCWM.

potent to interfere at such a distance as long as things go well for the Arabs."[6] The situation was no different in 1879. It is possible that Barghash might even have been satisfied with retaining Abdulla bin Nasibu as his *liwali;* his normal reply to Kirk, when he was pushed by his overpowerful adviser into agreeing to policies that he really opposed, was to plead his inability to act, while at the same time reaffirming his devotion to Kirk's advice. Kirk could wish for a better *liwali,* one more suited to his policies, one who would "work with the native chiefs, the actual rulers of the country," but he was powerless to do more.

It was Southon's unpleasant task to explain this rather unsatisfying answer to Mirambo; unfortunately we do not possess the details of what must have been a lively conversation. The unresolved problem, however, was eased somewhat by the death of Said bin Salim in November 1879. Said bin Salim had increasingly felt himself a pawn in the hands of Mirambo; he had tried incessantly, using Southon's influence whenever possible, to receive permission to return to Zanzibar. But as long as Mirambo thought he was useful, he was kept in Uyui. Just before his death the British missionary Arthur Copplestone, sympathizing with his plight since the clever Arab had convinced many missionaries that his deposition was due to his open friendship for Europeans visiting Unyanyembe, described him as "a man driven to despair."[7] But Mirambo had no pity for his prisoner. With Said bin Salim's death, all concerned hoped that Abdulla bin Nasibu, freed from his justifiable fears of a counter coup, would moderate his intrigues against Mirambo. A significant period of quiet did follow, and Abdulla bin Nasibu, although still hostile to Mirambo, appeared content to avoid any direct interference in Urambo.

SOUTHON, PROTESTANT MISSIONARY

Southon, apart from the not too onerous political tasks Mirambo set him to, settled down to the missionary work which had

[6] Kirk to Foreign Office, Sept. 29, 1871, E-61, ZA.
[7] Copplestone to Wigram, Nov. 17, 1879, C.A6/09, CMS.

brought him to Urambo for the London Missionary Society. There were no outstanding difficulties. Right at the start of Southon's stay, in August 1879, Mirambo offered the missionary his choice of a location for a mission residence, plus aid from his followers in its construction. The mission station, about a two- or three-hour walk from Mirambo's new capital, was perhaps an indication that the African leader wanted to be spared any potentially bothersome details of Southon's Christian endeavors. Southon, however, never complained about the location. Far more important in his eyes, Mirambo listened attentively to his religious discussions. The *ntemi* once even stated a desire to send one of his sons to Britain for a Western education, although Southon eventually discovered that this was not a serious suggestion since Mirambo repeatedly thought up excuses to block any departure. One good reason, besides his political usefulness, for Mirambo's attentiveness was the medical skill of Southon. Shortly after his arrival Southon removed a troublesome nonmalignant tumor from Mirambo's arm and the operation impressed the doctor as much as it did the African chief. Southon reported, "I wished to chloroform him but he assured me he could stand the pain, so I made no demur. He stood the operation with a stoicism I much admired, never flinching or betraying any sign of feeling pain." When asked by the admiring Southon about the pain, Mirambo said he felt "only a very little," assuring his physician all had been "quite easy," and requesting the removal of two other tumors on his back. The bemused Southon put him off until he had studied the results of the first operation.

All of the events recounted above, plus the quick surrender of the loads lost by the Broyon-Dodgshun caravan, gave Southon full satisfaction. Officially, his visit to Urambo had been only an exploratory venture, designed to verify the suitability of its location and the temper of its ruler for the work of the London Missionary Society. Satisfied on all accounts, Southon left for Ujiji to report to the regional council of his mission. The journey was made easy by Mirambo. He ominously informed the African leader of Southon's caravan: "Tell the chiefs the white man is my brother and if they take so much as half a shukka from him, it won't be good for them." Showing concern for Southon, Mirambo counseled about his expected return, "Don't come in the rain or you will get sick."[8] Hearing Southon's descriptions of his reception at Urambo his missionary brethren at Ujiji quickly authorized the permanent occupation of Mirambo's capital, a decision which was enthusiastically accepted by the society's directors in London.

Southon returned to Urambo in September 1879 to begin his work. He remained at his station without a European companion for nearly a year, his daily tasks made easier by a few Muslim coastmen who labored for the missionary without troubling themselves concerning his Christian beliefs. Relations with Mirambo continued satisfactory, although frustrating, since, despite the ruler's frequent promises, no youths were sent to Southon's proposed school. Mirambo's conduct seems puzzling; normally he was most receptive to measures which might lead to the advancement of his people. Justifiably impressed by Southon's medical skills, Mirambo had encouraged his resident missionary's hopes. "He is eager for his people to be taught medicine," reported Southon, "and even thinks I ought to take more than one lad to make a doctor of."[9] Perhaps Mirambo's failure to accept the opportunities offered by Southon, the teacher, was based on reasoning roughly similar to that which Steven Feierman has postulated for Kimweri ya Nyumbai, the powerful ruler of the Shambaa of Tanzania (he died in the 1860's); that the African leader attempted to keep everyone but himself isolated from foreign contacts to ensure his paramountcy within his state.[10]

Whatever the reason, Southon was unable to open a school until October 1881; even then it did not function efficiently because of the irregular attendance of the youths from chiefly families who constituted most of the pupils. One of Mirambo's sons participated for a time; when he ceased attending the warrior leader of Urambo merely said that the lad was beyond his control,

8 Southon's Journal, Sept. 7-Oct. 26, 1879, entry of Sept. 8, 1879, Journals: Central Africa, 1879-1880, CCWM.

9 Southon to Whitehouse, Jan. 21, 1880, Central Africa, 1880, CCWM.

10 Steven Feierman, "The Shambaa," in Andrew Roberts, ed., Tanzania Before 1900 (Nairobi, 1968), 11.

and he could do nothing with him.[11] The problem was a lasting one in Urambo and Southon's successor achieved some success with his school only by paying pupils to attend.

The school failure did not damage the relationship between Southon and Mirambo. A principal reason for this was the missionary's refusal to make bitter protestations against such hindrances to missionary work; rather, he kept busy at whatever useful tasks he could perform with the hope that eventually Mirambo would come around to be interested in the Christian message, if not for himself, then at least for his people. Mirambo and his important subordinates continually visited the busy missionary, observing with admiration his varied practical skills, and hoping to learn some of them. Or, when needing help for his commercial dealings at the coast, Mirambo went to Southon, hoping to avoid more imbroglios of the Broyon-Morton kind. Southon advised that Mirambo should not continually pester Kirk to supervise his men when they arrived in Zanzibar with ivory to barter. He counseled Mirambo instead to begin a permanent commercial arrangement with an important European merchant house—Southon naturally supplied him with the name of a British firm. Mirambo was pleased with the suggestion, although it does not appear that he made continuous use of such an arrangement in the future. Two incidents indicative of Southon's local standing can be cited. Mirambo once invited Southon to admire his skill with firearms. Southon noted that "at 250 yards he could hit an anthill about three feet high." The missionary was a much better shot and he went on to demonstrate it before Mirambo's followers. The *ntemi* showed no offence at his second place in this contest of talents.[12] The second has to do with an offer from Mirambo that Southon serve as temporary chief of Urambo's capital while he was absent conducting a campaign. Southon refused—not wishing to be drawn into the details of local politics (this was one of the cardinal principles of the

11 Southon to Thompson, Dec. 31, 1881, Reports: Central Africa, 1880-1890, CCWM.

12 Southon's Journal, Oct. 27-Nov. 30, 1879, entry of Nov. 21, 1879, Journals: Central Africa, 1878-1880, CCWM.

London Missionary Society)—without damaging his reputation with the Nyamwezi *ntemi.*

But even with the pressure of his many labors to occupy his attention, it was a lonely life for Southon, cut off from most of the aspects of his own civilization. And close contact with the Nyamwezi in general could not replace the loss since Southon found the learning of their language a slow process. It was, he said, "exceedingly difficult to Europeans on account of the gutteral accent which prevails in it."[13] In an amusing—if pathetic— exchange of letters with Kirk and his wife, Southon wrote asking for their aid in securing for him a wife suitable to help in his missionary work. Southon explained that he was willing to leave the details of the search to Mrs. Kirk, stating that "I am willing to take my chance of getting an unsuitable partner, for is not marriage a lottery with more blanks than prizes?" He added ruefully, "Very unpoetical is it not? But C. Africa knocks all the poetry out and puts in common sense." Notwithstanding this request, plus later ones, the lonely missionary finished his life as a bachelor.

[13] Southon to Whitehouse, Nov. 1, 1879, Central Africa, 1879, CCWM.

VI

MIRAMBO AND THE
CARTER-CADENHEAD AFFAIR

PROBLEMS OVER KAREMA

WHILE MIRAMBO was enjoying an unclouded relationship with his British friends, working through the intermediary of his unofficial but nevertheless useful missionary resident, he was not having a similarly favorable experience with the Belgian members of the International African Association. Lieutenant Cambier, after reaching Unyanyembe from Urambo, had no thoughts of ever returning to Mirambo's capital; "I could not," he informed the French consul in Zanzibar, "establish myself with a bandit of this kind."[1] Moreover he had received new orders from Brussels directing him to found the association's initial East African station on the eastern shore of Lake Tanganyika, to the south of Ujiji. The orders stemmed from the advice of Henry Stanley who, after Britain had demonstrated no official interest in his discoveries made during his 1874-77 expedition to the mouth of the Congo River, had entered the employ of Leopold to begin the work ultimately leading to the formation of the Congo Independent State. En route from Unyanyembe to his designated goal Cambier stopped at the populous center of the Nyamwezi leader, Simba, located in Usawila among the Konongo peoples, where he met one of the most successful leaders of the

[1] Cambier to de Freycinet, Jan. 30, 1879, in de Freycinet to M.A.E., March 5, 1879, Correspondance Commerciale, Zanzibar, Archives des Affaires Etrangères, Paris.

wandering bands of elephant hunters then spread throughout eastern Africa. This individual, Matumera, transferred to Cambier the ownership of the village of Karema, in the territory of the Bende people, a center he had recently acquired through a successful campaign. When Cambier arrived at the lakeside location he found a small and undistinguished village, but with a trained military disposition he obeyed orders and set to work building a strongly fortified station.

Mirambo was extremely displeased when he learned about Cambier's establishment at Karema. In a conversation with a passing missionary, Edward Hore, he vehemently complained, first about Cambier's rush to leave Urambo, and then about the building at Karema, a location which he asserted was part of his dominions. Mirambo said bluntly: "Cambier treated me badly—he was a fool."[2] Still aroused, Mirambo requested the surprised Hore to carry a formal complaint to the Belgian representative in Zanzibar, but the London Missionary Society man refused this involvement in politics, and the complaint was forwarded instead through Hore's follower, Juma Nasibu. If the message ever reached Zanzibar nothing came of it, and Mirambo was left to nurse his anger about Cambier's presence at Karema.

Cambier remained in command at the Lake Tanganyika station until December 1880. With the assistance of subsequent arrivals of Belgian officers, building continued at Karema. Other association plans for new stations located across Lake Tanganyika on the route to the upper Congo River were blocked by deaths among the very limited personnel of the organization in East Africa. The busy officers, working far from any tangible evidence of Mirambo's claims of sovereignty—he had, it appears, no real control over the Karema region—continued their tasks without overly concerning themselves with the Nyamwezi leader. But Mirambo, well informed of all their proceedings, did not forget the Belgians; his continuing unhappiness at their actions became a significant contributory factor to one of the most unfortunate events of his career.

2 Hore to Whitehouse, Nov. 30, 1880, Central Africa, 1878-1880, CCWM.

TRAGEDY AT MPIMBWE

King Leopold, while his officers worked diligently to make Karema a safe and flourishing station, was developing new schemes to further his African designs. He decided to support an important experiment to improve the East African transport system. All attempts to replace the existing inadequate method of human carriage of loads along the narrow paths of the interior had so far failed, but in the late 1870's many concerned individuals of all nationalities had begun thinking of one seemingly obvious solution to the problem, the utilization of the African elephant. The Belgian ruler, perhaps motivated by the first-hand experiences of an earlier visit to Ceylon, resolved to support a trial expedition which would test the suitability of Indian elephants for work in Africa. If these beasts could work efficiently in East Africa, then the next step of the experiment called for the capture and training of African elephants. (There were then no trained African elephants.) Leopold ruled that the venture be conducted under his personal direction, and not under the rubric of the International African Association, a fateful decision, as it turned out, since the mission worked under the unfamiliar Belgian flag instead of that of the association. A Briton with the necessary experience, including the language skills required to work with Indian elephant handlers (mahouts), was chosen as the expedition's commander. Frederick Carter was a very popular personality, quickly making many friends in East Africa, especially among the British community. To the Scots explorer Joseph Thomson he was, in a typical reaction, "a fine, warm-hearted Irishman, ready to face any hardships or danger, full of anecdote and humour, and of the most buoyant temperament." The ready affection felt by all for Carter was a matter of significance for Mirambo's future relationship with the British.

Four Indian elephants were landed near Dar es Salaam in July 1879, and with each one of them carrying a thousand-pound load, Carter led his expedition forth on the march to Karema. En route, Carter noted, he was informed that Mirambo, as ever much interested in better ways of travel, had sent him gifts in an effort to induce the elephant leader to settle in his territory. But there was no personal contact between Carter and Mirambo, and the leader of Leopold's venture does not appear to have paid much attention to Mirambo's reported offer. Only one elephant reached the Lake Tanganyika goal alive in December 1879, although another beast died in sight of Karema. Nevertheless Carter, an ebullient optimist, steadfastly held the experiment a success; he explained the deaths as due to the adverse conditions in a new and unknown environment. Carter organized plans for further experiments with elephants, including the use of experienced Asian animals, to establish a training center on the Indian model for East African elephants. More investigatory work was needed, however.

Carter, during the difficult trip to Karema, had suffered the usual troubles of a European traveler in East Africa from African leaders demanding payment for passage and for provisions. He had also followed a route containing several very difficult types of terrain for elephant travel. Both these experiences made Carter especially anxious to avoid Ugogo on any future expedition; he fully accepted Edward Hore's 1878 description of that African people as the "hongo squeezing Wagogo." With the assistance of a fresh recruit, the Scot Tom Cadenhead, a long-time friend of Carter who joined him at Karema, the British officer decided to try out a new route to the East African coast which, if it proved easily passable, might improve the chances of success for future elephant work. The route chosen lay to the south of the normal Unyanyembe-Lake Tanganyika path of travel, roughly following the seventh parallel of latitude. Carter and Cadenhead set forth from Karema in June 1880, leading a moderate-sized expedition, and flying the Belgian flag. They had heard that their proposed path of march was unsettled because of hostilities between contending African groups; Joseph Thomson, traveling in that region about six weeks previous to their departure, had written from the village of Simba warning the two men to follow a different route. But in that era of East African travel any route could become dangerous at very little notice, and Carter and Cadenhead, ignoring the advice, marched off on their last journey.

Meantime, while Carter organized his return expedition, Mirambo was busily planning a new campaign. It turned out to be the most fateful campaign since Mirambo's decision of the early 1870's to challenge the Arabs of Unyanyembe. In June 1880 he led his forces from Urambo to fight against the ruler of the village of Nsagula, located in the region south of the Ugala River. No battle ensued since the designated enemies were so fearful of Mirambo that they fled at the news of his coming. But the Nyamwezi war leader, Simba of Usawila, seized the opportunity to seek, and gain, the support of Mirambo's army for a joint campaign against one of his rivals, Kasogera, the Nyamwezi leader of Mpimbwe, a village situated in the territory of the Pimbwe people who lived to the north of Lake Rukwa. Shortly before the arrival of the Mirambo-Simba forces at Mpimbwe, Carter's party, on June 23, 1880, reached the village.

Kasogera, aware of the forthcoming attack planned against his center, moved rapidly to attempt to secure the chance European arrivals as allies. He hoped they would either prevent an assault on the village, or participate in Mpimbwe's defense if the hostilities did occur. He informed Carter of the Mirambo-Simba advance and insisted that the British traveler's party enter Mpimbwe. Carter, who had a reputation as a man of peace, refused; there was no advantage to be gained from assisting Kasogera. But the chief, desperate for assistance, informed Carter that a refusal would cause him to consider the British-led group as allies of Mirambo and Simba. Thus an immediate attack on their camp would follow. Carter, trapped in an impossible situation, discussed their plight with the African leaders of his expedition. Their counsel was to enter Mpimbwe since they believed that Mirambo and Simba were not yet in the environs of the center. The Africans obviously wished to temporize in an effort to avoid a crisis; later they hoped to receive permission to leave Mpimbwe before any fighting began. Carter, while unhappy at this plan, realized that he could not rely upon his African followers to support any firm line of conduct he might propose against Kasogera; he also had to face the unpleasant truth that the supply of water his followers badly needed was located within Mpimbwe's walls. Nevertheless Carter argued on, vainly attempting to convince his cowed men that they would be hopelessly trapped once they placed themselves under Kasogera's super-

vision in Mpimbwe. But the arguments, however logical, made
no impression on his unreceptive listeners. Meanwhile Kasogera
organized a threatening demonstration to help force a decision.
Realizing at last that his men planned to desert if he did not
capitulate to Kasogera and enter the village, Carter submitted,
leading the expedition to a camp site in Mpimbwe. On the next
morning, June 24, Carter's forebodings proved true; the worried
Kasogera refused to allow the expedition to leave Mpimbwe.

The men of Simba and Mirambo struck the apprehensive village that same day. Kasogera and his people offered almost no
resistance to the attacking warriors; they fled as the Urambo
army, with its usual efficiency, quickly overran Mpimbwe's fortifications. Carter unhappily found his expedition in the midst
of passing bands of the battle-excited invaders. Striving to avoid
presenting any cause for them to attack his position, Carter
hoisted a white flag and quietly waited with his men. Initially
the incoming warriors rushed past the camp without notice, apparently more concerned with securing the victory and collecting
the spoils abandoned by the Mpimbwe inhabitants. But finally
one band of the invaders opened fire, without any provocation,
upon the closely grouped, passive expedition; when Cadenhead,
unable to remain quiet any longer, returned the fire, he was
immediately shot and killed. The expedition then broke up in
panic, the men fleeing in all directions, leaving Carter with a few
remaining followers to make an organized attempt to leave
Mpimbwe. This group, firing as they marched, managed to reach
the outskirts of the village, but the sporadic skirmishing necessary
for the move exhausted their ammunition. Carter either was
killed by the warriors of Mirambo and Simba or, fearing capture,
he committed suicide. It should be noted that we have the information for the Mpimbwe affair largely from Carter himself; the
leader of the expedition kept up his journal, which survived the
debacle, to within two hours of his death. Many of Carter's
African followers escaped; 80 of the original 150 men of the
caravan reached Karema not too long after the battle, and relatively few of the remainder were killed. They were either taken
prisoner by Mirambo and Simba or managed to reach safety in
the villages between Mpimbwe and Unyanyembe. These men

quickly spread the first news of the tragedy to the various Europeans then present in that part of Africa.

THE REPERCUSSIONS OF MPIMBWE

It was a shattering message. Was the powerful Mirambo, heretofore the trusted friend of most Europeans, and the particular friend of the influential John Kirk, guilty of a premeditated attack on a peaceful expedition led by two Britons? The decision as to Mirambo's guilt or innocence would determine whether the Urambo *ntemi* would continue to receive British support for the greater extension of his authority throughout Unyamwezi and its neighboring regions.

The stunned members of the International African Association, who all along had been fearful of Mirambo because of his treatment of Cambier and his claims to sovereignty over Karema, first interviewed the disorganized survivors of Carter's expedition. These Belgian officers had no doubt that Mirambo was wholly responsible for the deaths. Captain Emile Popelin, an intelligent and capable officer, was the Belgian most involved in the interviews. Popelin had learned before the attack on Mpimbwe of the dangers facing Carter and Cadenhead because of Mirambo's campaigning on their proposed route; he had rushed from Karema to try to divert them from the war zone. His small force had been unable to get through, and in danger from the many undisciplined marauding war bands on the caravan routes, Popelin went for refuge to Unyanyembe. There, amidst unsettling rumors of Mirambo's movements after Mpimbwe—the Arabs feared he might even attack Unyanyembe—Popelin was present to interview many of Carter's fugitive followers. According to the information that he gained, Mirambo had known of the presence of the two Europeans in Mpimbwe. Thus, Popelin reasoned, if the powerful Nyamwezi leader had wanted to exercise his authority he could have prevented their deaths. But instead Mirambo had let his men precipitate hostilities with Carter's peaceful group even though, it was claimed, he was not far from the actual scene of the fighting when Carter entered Mpimbwe. Later Popelin interviewed one survivor, Muhammad, who had remained with

Carter right to the moment of his leader's death; he corroborated Popelin's previous findings. Popelin's Belgian companions at Karema, from their own researches, generally supported his interpretation of the events at Mpimbwe.

An entirely different view of the responsibility for the deaths of Carter and Cadenhead came from Ebenezer Southon at Urambo. He had been appalled at hearing the news from Mpimbwe, waiting nervously for Mirambo's return to hear his version of events. According to the British missionary, as soon as Mirambo realized that two Britons had been killed as a result of the storming of Mpimbwe he had hurried back to his capital. He did so, Mirambo informed Southon, "in order that you may tell the English Consul how sorry I am about this sad business and how anxious I am to give him a full account of how it happened." Mirambo explained to Southon that he had no knowledge of the presence of Carter, Cadenhead, or their expedition, in Mpimbwe; he had learned of them only upon finding their bodies when he entered the captured village. In another version from Urambo, Mirambo, who had been at the rear of his troops, learned of their presence when a lieutenant rushed up to say that there were Europeans in Mpimbwe; Mirambo claimed that he immediately issued orders to spare them, and to rescue them, but his effort was too late. In either case their deaths were accordingly merely a most unfortunate and unavoidable accident of war. Southon reported that Mirambo was most upset over the tragedy; he had been heard to lament to an African companion: "I have been trying to convince the English that I am their true friend and have done my best to be friendly towards them, but now that this loss has happened what will they think of me?" Given a free hand by Mirambo to do so, Southon conducted his own investigations among the survivors of Mpimbwe, gathering as complete a record as was possible to forward to Kirk. He also returned the remaining materials of the expedition given to him by Mirambo, including Carter's journal, to Zanzibar. Southon's conclusions were most positive: Mirambo did not know Carter and Cadenhead were in Mpimbwe and he bore no personal responsibility for their deaths. To buttress his proofs Southon also convinced Mirambo to send along one of his chief subordinates, Magangira, to Kirk so that the British official might hear directly from him Mirambo's own story.

All the collected information about the events at Mpimbwe, from Popelin, Southon, and many other sources, was quickly sent to Zanzibar where the crucial decision, that of John Kirk, had to be made regarding Mirambo's responsibility. Any step the Sultan of Zanzibar would take in the affair depended entirely upon Kirk's interpretation of Mirambo's role. The first information which Kirk received, from two survivors of Carter's party, was hostile to Mirambo. From it Kirk decided that this campaign of Mirambo's had been designed to place all of the trade routes passing from Unyanyembe to Lake Tanganyika under his authority. Carter, meantime, while unaware of Mirambo's plans, was attempting to open a wholly new route to the East African coast, one which would have been independent of Mirambo's control. Mirambo, Kirk concluded, knew of Carter's intentions, and "this . . . was exactly what Mirambo had set himself to stop." To Kirk, who when he gave advice expected it to be followed, this was all the more disturbing since, Kirk claimed, he had been for some time past advising Mirambo against just such a campaign. His advice instead had been for Mirambo to remain at peace, while working closely with Southon, to make his already extensive possessions so secure that all trade would naturally flow through them rather than through Arab-dominated areas.

And Kirk was further aroused since he maintained that Mirambo had knowingly abused his efforts to keep the Arabs of Unyanyembe at peace with him, that realizing he was free from danger from Unyanyembe, Mirambo had undertaken this campaign. Kirk's efforts with the Arabs, pursued since about 1878, had been extensive. Fearing that Mirambo planned a campaign against them, although this information was probably false, Kirk attempted to take advantage of the changed conditions following Said bin Salim's death to resolve all the problems between Unyanyembe and Urambo. In March 1880 Kirk had Sultan Barghash send a representative to Unyanyembe to hold talks with Abdulla bin Nasibu concerning his grievances against Mirambo; the delegate was next supposed to visit Urambo to hear the other side of the story. But the delegate became ill and refused to leave Unyanyembe, sending instead a local Arab to Mirambo. Instead of working for peace he spent most of his time talking against the British, who, he said, would eventually seize Urambo. Mirambo recognized his duplicity and sent his own delegates to Unyanyembe to present his case to Barghash's representative. The reports from this potentially useful diplomatic mission are not known, and the events at Mpimbwe caused the mission to be quickly forgotten.

Southon too received a share of Kirk's displeasure. Kirk judged that, because of the missionary's influential position in Urambo, he must have known the goal of Mirambo's campaign, and therefore should have clearly stated to Mirambo that he was violating the main lines of Kirk's counsel. Subsequent information reaching Kirk about Mpimbwe, particularly from Juma Nasibu, who had been his African informant in the earlier Broyon difficulties with Mirambo, substantiated his conclusions. The most damaging blow to Mirambo's interpretation of the deaths came in September when Kirk learned from new indigenous sources that Mirambo had dispatched spies to report on Mpimbwe the day before the battle. Thus, he concluded, Mirambo must have known that the Europeans were there. Kirk even went one step further in his allocation of guilt: since some Nyamwezi war bands had passed Carter and Cadenhead without inaugurating hostilities, those who actually attacked the Europeans must have done so upon receiving direct orders from Mirambo. Kirk's conclusion was inescapable: Mirambo was personally responsible for the tragedy.

Because of his predominant influence in Zanzibar, Kirk's strong views appeared to be of special significance when it suddenly became very likely that a significant combination of military forces would be dispatched inland to punish Mirambo for his supposed guilt. The men of the International African Association, the Arabs of Unyanyembe, and Sultan Barghash's new modern army (formed after 1875), all were reported poised for action. The Belgians were naturally the quickest to react. A new expedition of the association destined for Karema under the command of Captain Guillaume Ramaeckers, with the first expedition of the German branch of the International African Association to East Africa following close behind it, had left the coast in July 1880. On their march they received the news of the Mpimbwe episode, along with disturbing rumors that Mirambo's warriors, in a continuation of the campaign, had raided the territory right up to Karema, destroying the station and killing its commander, Cambier. Reinforcements were rushed quickly to Ramaeckers from the Sultan of Zanzibar, increasing the association's strength to 400 men, along with a machine gun—possibly the first to be sent into the East African interior—recently sent as a gift from Leopold to Barghash. But despite their apprehension, the Belgians and Germans proceeded inland without involvement with Mirambo, their worries being further moderated by learning in August that Karema had not been attacked. They reached Unyanyembe in safety, where the Germans left the group to found their station in Ugunda. The Belgians continued peacefully to Karema, and planning no offensive action to avenge Carter and Cadenhead, they left the resolution of the problem of Mirambo to the Zanzibar authorities.

Kirk, who normally reported everything of possible concern to British interests in East Africa to the Foreign Office, was strangely silent during this troubled period. This conduct leads to the suspicion that some action might have been planned in Zanzibar against Mirambo, measures Kirk could have claimed that Sultan Barghash never informed him of. But it was clear that something was afoot. In August, Kirk wrote to Southon warning him of the potential dangers of an Arab-Mirambo war. "It is not to be supposed," said Kirk, "that the Zanzibar authorities will permit their position and the trade with the interior to be thus interfered with by one native chief without resistance nor will the nations of Europe who now take an interest in developing the resources of Africa and the welfare of the people rest quiet while their subjects and their agents are thus butchered to serve the ends and gratify the ambition of one individual."[3] Southon also had other indications of approaching trouble; he wrote in his diary on November 10, 1880, that he had heard

[3] Southon to Whitehouse, Nov. 29, 1880, enclosing Kirk to Southon, Aug. 12, 1880, CCWM.

"Barghash has declared war against Mirambo and there are 7000 men at Mamboia [near Mpwapwa] to fight him!" Then in December, Mirambo offered to provide an escort for the London Missionary Society men—Southon now had a companion, David Williams—to the coast so that they would avoid the oncoming hostilities.

The home authorities of the London Missionary Society and the Church Missionary Society reacted vigorously to the possible dangers of war, fearing for the personal safety of their missionaries and for the continuance of their work at Uyui and Urambo. Both the Christian groups contacted the Foreign Office to make known their objections to any military ventures against Mirambo by Sultan Barghash—and Kirk. The missionary directors called instead for a thorough investigation to precede any such move. After all, they reasoned, had not Mirambo in his previous career shown consistent friendship for Europeans? Their views were embodied in a joint memorial to the Foreign Office, with Edward Hutchinson of the Church Missionary Society emphasizing that "the maintenance of friendly relations with this chief Mirambo appears to be of much importance to the highest interests of the natives of the country and also to the development and opening up of the interior to legitimate trade and the introduction of civilization." Hutchinson continued that his information, drawn from missionaries, did not uphold Kirk's views of Mirambo's guilt, and that the African leader's campaigns were not disruptive to commerce; instead they were undertaken with the goal of "improving the means of communication with the vast country over which he is supreme chief," an aim originally encouraged by Kirk. Thus Hutchinson forcefully concluded, "any hostile movement of the Sultan of Zanzibar against Mirambo [should be condemned] as being unjust and uncalled for and likely to lead to most disastrous results."

The Church Missionary Society was a bit taken aback when Kirk subsequently informed them that one of their most experienced men, Charles Stokes, held Mirambo responsible for the deaths of Carter and Cadenhead, while describing the Urambo *ntemi* as "a deep dyed villain." That Stokes later changed his opinion made little impression upon Kirk. Stokes' turnabout resulted from his learning from African sources that Mirambo, for once, had been in the rear of his troops at Mpimbwe, not in the forefront, and thus he was unaware of the happenings in the village. Because of this information Stokes, who had encountered another headman of Mirambo's en route to Zanzibar to explain the affair to all in authority who would listen, provided the African with a letter of introduction to Kirk. The British official was not interested, even when the concerned missionary later urged, "You will find out your own [former] policy is the best, Mirambo has been your friend and don't desert him without proof of his guilt. If you lived up country . . . you would find out a man like Mirambo was required to keep the lawless Arabs in check."

When the missionary memorial was forwarded to Kirk by a questioning Foreign Office, he met the charges head on. Kirk utterly rejected the two societies' description of Mirambo's campaign, affirming that it was impossible "to separate the main incident from the destruction and plunder of the Expedition . . . and the conduct of a desolating war undertaken without apparent justification for the sole object of stopping rival trade routes." And, Kirk added, all this was accompanied with widespread slave raiding and the taking of plunder. He remained adamant on Mirambo's guilt, even speaking against Southon's aid in the dispatch of Mirambo's headman to him; this, charged Kirk, was merely an ill-concealed espionage venture by Mirambo designed to check upon the effects of Mpimbwe in Zanzibar and to learn how the sultan planned to react. An indication of Kirk's displeasure with Southon was also given in a conversation he had with the Belgian representative in Zanzibar; the official reported that he characterized the missionary as "un mauvais homme." With apparent regret, Kirk concluded in his answer to the missionary societies, "To me, I may say, it is a sad disappointment to give up the hope that under good advice Mirambo might be content to raise and extend his influence in a more legitimate way for the power and prestige his name now carries with it would have been of incalculable service." Nevertheless, to Kirk, Mirambo had made his choice on how to follow the advice coming from Zanzibar, and the best policy thus to follow in the future was for the sultan to rely upon his Arab and Indian subjects to keep the interior secure. In brief, Kirk was returning to his original policy, the one he had followed before Mirambo had first drawn him away from the tried policy of exclusive reliance upon Zanzibar.

Concerning the alleged planned military operations by the sultan referred to by his questioners, Kirk summarily denied their existence. The ruler of Zanzibar, Kirk testily explained, had undertaken a limited movement inland, but this had been resolved upon before the Mpimbwe affair, and it was only indirectly stimulated by the later deaths of Penrose, Carter, and Cadenhead, which were all really only incidents in "a general malaise in the interior" which affected the interests of the sultan and his subjects. The Belgians, Kirk went on, had made their initial warlike moves, with the sultan's consent, to ensure the protection of their own men, and therefore he had felt it his duty to warn the missionaries of potential hostilities which might threaten their safety. And, Kirk waxed strongly, as far as he knew the sultan never had any plans at all to strike against Mirambo; on the contrary, he did his utmost to restrain the Unyanyembe Arabs from taking any initiative since he knew from past experience that they probably would be defeated. In fact, Barghash's only hostile move toward Mirambo had been to detain a large caravan carrying gunpowder which was ready to leave for Urambo; other goods belonging to that chief, including some load of firearms, had not been interfered with.

Since these events, Kirk continued, Sultan Barghash had taken some important positive measures to bring stability to East Africa. He had forbidden the sale of gunpowder on the coast as a principal way of influencing the harmful actions of interior African chiefs. Kirk did not explain why, if any of the sultan's edicts on gunpowder sales were effective, he had to keep reissuing them. Nor did he mention, as did the German naturalist Richard Böhm, that as late as May 1880 a tacit arrangement had been in operation along the coast allowing Mirambo's followers to barter ivory for gunpowder and other goods. More to the point, Kirk reported that Barghash had decided to take steps to protect the main trade route to Unyanyembe; a fort had been built at

Mamboya and additional measures were planned for Ugogo. This was a politically significant advance of the inland authority of Zanzibar since the sultan's previous most inland bases had been located by the Kingani River near Bagamoyo. Not one of these moves, however, was happening anywhere near Urambo or Unyanyembe, so Kirk said there was no cause to fear hostilities. "On Mirambo himself," Kirk moralized, "the fact that his recent conduct has been condemned and his supply of powder cut off has begun to produce a salutary effect and there is good reason to hope that under such an influence as Mr. Southon may be able to exert he will come to see that the line of action I had before urged upon him is the best and that without the use of violence he could gain a far greater influence and attract traders to pass through and settle in his district in preference to going elsewhere or taking other routes." For the present Kirk promised that he would deal with Mirambo only through Southon, "a course that seems likely to pave the way for useful intervention at some future time." Finally, Kirk stated his hope for the course of his new policy: "My ultimate hope is that should the Sultan of Zanzibar succeed in opening the road through Ugogo Mirambo may then, seeing His Highness' power not far off, and feeling by that time the effect of the stoppage of gun powder and perhaps also of arms be ready to join in a common action for securing the safety of roads from the coast to the interior."

With his course of action to Mirambo and to Barghash explained, Kirk asked the Foreign Office for a ruling on his proceedings. If, he explained, the sultan was to follow a more active role in the interior he had to know exactly how much British support he could depend upon. If left entirely to his own decisions, with the British maintaining that Mirambo was an independent ruler outside Zanzibar's sphere of influence, Barghash might, Kirk reasoned, ultimately "feel himself absolved from taking notice of the doings of his people outside the limits placed by us upon his authority." The officials of the Foreign Office, as usual, had no interests in firm commitments in inland East Africa. Kirk was vaguely instructed to follow the policy "best calculated to prevent hostilities and maintain friendly relations between the Sultan and Mirambo and between the latter chief and travellers within the districts over which he claims to exercise authority." As for the sultan, Kirk received more positive instructions; he was "to avoid committing Her Majesty's Government to any policy entailing a definition of the extent of the Sultan's territory inland." Thus the future details of the relationship between Barghash and Mirambo were largely left to Kirk. As will appear, this determined official never reversed his attitude toward the Nyamwezi ruler.

With documents crossing furiously between London and Zanzibar, and with the African interior beset by numerous rumors, it was not surprising that Mirambo was concerned and that the missionaries living near to him, Southon at Urambo and Arthur Copplestone and George Litchfield at Uyui, feared the worst. From the men of the Church Missionary Society in Buganda came the news that Mutesa was ready to join with the Arabs in a campaign against Mirambo. Edward Hore, from Ujiji, reported that the Arabs living there were in panic because they feared that Mirambo would strike to destroy their center before Barghash's army, rumored to have 7000 men, advanced from the coast. And when Kirk wrote to Southon that coming events in the interior "will clearly effect your personal safety and the prospects of the mission," and "it is therefore my duty in the present position of affairs to ask you as the representative of an English Mission to be most careful so as not to compromise your safety during the conflict that is certain to ensue," the message was certainly clear and foreboding, particularly since Kirk closed by stating that if Southon remained in Urambo he would be caught "in the course of a native war in which the sympathy and support of the civilized world will be against Mirambo and his allies." Kirk conveyed the same warning to Copplestone at Uyui, adding, Copplestone said, that "war will be declared by Seyd Barghash against Mirambo [and] carried on regular native fashion." Although worried, all the missionaries decided to remain at their posts in Mirambo's territories, recognizing that to be a missionary meant facing risks and that any hurried evacuation could end all the influence they had striven so hard to build for their societies with the people of Urambo and Uyui, these reasons forming what Southon described as "his duty and inclination."

The fears of the missionaries were ended when Kirk wrote to Southon in January 1881 that there would be no war. He added that Mirambo, in his messages to Zanzibar, had "practically admitted that he was the author of the murder of Carter." Kirk informed Southon that he now considered that Mirambo had seen the error of his expansionist policy, and that for himself, "I still hold to supporting native states and chiefs, but Mirambo in his present power seems a dangerous man and likely to do more harm than good." Southon had to accept this interpretation, no matter how much he contested Kirk's opinions concerning Mirambo. He replied to the consul that he would do his best to continue working for British interests, proving his assertion by explaining that he had not invited the French trader Emile Sergère (to be discussed below) to visit Urambo when that adventurous individual had written to him for permission. Instead, Southon said, he was working to keep the Urambo market open for any British traders who might find it possible to reside there.

For whatever reasons, war never came. The Arabs of Unyanyembe, even though it was reported that they had sent to Zanzibar for war materials so that they might act against Mirambo, had no inclination to fight with their more powerful former opponent. They certainly were not going to wage war to avenge the deaths of two Europeans unless as part of a broader coalition which when victorious would bring them commercial and political advantage. The forces that Sultan Barghash dispatched into the interior, under the direction of his British commander-in-chief, Lloyd Mathews, probably were the explanation for the rumors of an advancing Zanzibar army of 7000 men, but in reality there were only a few hundred. They proceeded inland only as far as Mamboya. There the soldiers constructed a fort, leaving on their return to Zanzibar merely a small garrison to serve as an occupying force and to intercept gunpowder supplies on the way to Urambo. There are a few indications that Mathews's troops hoped to project a line of stations farther into the interior, plans which were wrecked by dissension among the unwilling African soldiers, but this information is not certain. One other cause of trouble with Mirambo was a reward of 50,000 francs reportedly offered by Sultan Barghash for Mirambo's head, but the Belgian consul alone recorded this information. After assessing the foregoing events, this author remains suspicious that Kirk, in his anger at Mirambo for disregarding his advice and for causing the death of his friend Frederick Carter, might have pressured the sultan to attempt some form of retaliation against Mirambo, a tentative course which was quickly shelved when questions concerning hostilities were asked in London. It would have been natural for the aroused Kirk to do this. In nineteenth-century European thinking the deaths of Europeans had to be avenged whenever possible to prevent the numerically superior Africans from thinking that they could kill Europeans with impunity. The Belgian officer Popelin had put his appeal for action to Kirk in exactly these terms. And if another tragedy did happen, Kirk's superiors in London might be all too ready to put the blame on him. Africans did take note of the failure to punish Mirambo for the deaths of Carter and Cadenhead. Years later the redoubtable Nyamwezi ruler of Katanga, Msiri, casually told a European missionary, "Oh, out East near Unyanyembe we killed several [Europeans],"[4] but Africans continued to be as tolerant of Europeans as they had been before the Mpimbwe affair.

In reviewing the events leading to the Mpimbwe tragedy, where does the question of Mirambo's guilt or innocence stand? Which opinion was closer to the truth—Mirambo's, Kirk's, Southon's, Popelin's? Past analyses of the deaths of Carter and Cadenhead, those of Alison Smith and Roland J. Harvey, support the explanations of Mirambo as supported by Southon and others; they maintain that Mirambo was not directly responsible for the deaths which they instead blame on the inherent difficulties of controlling aroused warriors in the heat of a battle. These difficulties were certainly present. Nevertheless, this author does not accept this interpretation. The material discussed in this volume amply demonstrates Mirambo's hostility to the members of the International African Association. More important, there is sufficient proof, collected by Kirk and the Belgians, to demonstrate that Mirambo had to be aware that there were

4 D. Crawford, *Thinking Black* (New York, 1913), 257.

Europeans in Mpimbwe when his forces arrived to storm the village. Yet this does not mean that Mirambo's regret for the tragedy was feigned; perhaps he learned then that the dead Europeans were Britons, fellow subjects of John Kirk, and not Belgians, despite the flag they flew. But even this explanation can be challenged. Carter and Cadenhead, particularly the former, were familiar figures in the region, and if Europeans were known to be in Mpimbwe, the connection must have been obvious. Finally, whether Mirambo knew the identity of the two Europeans or not, he alone must bear the responsibility for the grievous miscalculation which cost him the support, which he had so carefully worked for, of the British representative in Zanzibar. If the resulting change in British policy was not a major blow to the plans of Mirambo himself in the last years of his life, it nevertheless was important for the future of Urambo. If the relations encouraged by Southon had flourished, to be continued by others after his death, while Kirk in Zanzibar had continued to demonstrate great interest in Mirambo's affairs, this situation could have provided a major influence for strengthening Mirambo's state when, after Mirambo's death, it most needed outside aid. With an influential European resident, in close ties with the authorities in Zanzibar, both British and Arab, the unfortunate succession of a weak ruler to follow Mirambo might not have led to the disintegration of Urambo before the German conquerors arrived to take control of Unyamwezi.

Mirambo understandably was greatly distressed by the change of attitude in Zanzibar, especially as expressed in the tightening of the gunpowder blockade enforced against his subjects. In the apparent hope of winning a change in that policy by a fait accompli, Mirambo sent down a party to Zanzibar to trade shortly after the difficulties at Mpimbwe. They found Kirk unchanging in attitude. Receiving no help at all from the British official, the Nyamwezi were left to trade on their own; unfamiliar with the mechanics of the market they left Zanzibar with little to show for Mirambo's venture. Mirambo did not accept Kirk's decision about their future relationship as final, however, and he intermittently tried during the remaining years of his life to return Kirk to his pre-Mpimbwe policies.

VII

THE LAST YEARS OF MIRAMBO

MIRAMBO'S CAMPAIGNS

To Mirambo the British connection to Urambo, although important, was not vital; he had created and developed his state using only his own talents and the available local resources. He did not plan to stop building now that one of his schemes to draw outside support had failed. Indeed, Mirambo was unable to change the normal course of his activities, for unless he kept his military force actively campaigning and consequently securing the spoils of war which they now expected, he would lose many of their number to other more successful war leaders, leaving Urambo at a serious military disadvantage against its enemies. Southon cogently wrote in 1879: "The Wanyamwezi at Urambo and the adjoining villages, are, for the most part, soldiers, who delight in war and bloodshed and who are led by a chief whose every thought is directed towards conquest, plunder and the acquisition of territory. Hence, where there occurs an opportunity, Mirambo and his 'Ruga Ruga' are constantly on the move and actually spend their whole time in planning, preparing for, or actually engaging in a war of greater or lesser magnitude." Some attention therefore must be devoted to this facet of Mirambo's career. But a detailed study of his campaigns must await the gathering of information relevant to the many areas in which he campaigned since the fragments we now have are often confusing and insufficient for a complete account.

After finishing in 1875 his inconclusive war with the Arabs, Mirambo appears to have made it his first business to attempt to win control of the territories through which traversed the caravan routes leading north from around Unyanyembe to Lake Victoria and its neighboring states, especially to Karagwe, the Haya state on the western side of the lake, and Buganda. His Arab enemies were not forgotten meantime. In November 1876 the Unyanyembe Arabs showed Shergold Smith 100 heads they claimed came from some of Mirambo's followers defeated during a skirmish near the center. But normally Mirambo left the Arabs in peace while he pursued campaigns destined in the long run to displace Unyanyembe as the principal commercial base of Un-yamwezi. During 1876 Mirambo gained about as much success in the Sukuma lands north of Unyamwezi as he ever would in the future. The ruler of the lakeside Zinza state of Bukara, Rwoma, a crafty individual who knew well how to protect his own inter-ests against his more powerful rivals, Mirambo and Mutesa of Buganda, was reported by Henry Stanley to be Mirambo's ally. The alliance probably covered little apart from general protesta-tions of friendship since Mirambo could never effectively contr Rwoma until he had Sukuma territory between their two sta firmly in hand. The two leaders even may have engaged in direct hostilities from time to time. Parts of 1877 and 1878 w spent by Mirambo in Sukuma territory, again without comp success, in seeking to attain domination through a serie raiding expeditions. As a practical matter, Mirambo's domin in this direction ended for all realistic purposes at Rwo borders.

Although Mirambo had not realized his ambitions in the tions of Lake Victoria, he had established a solid ba future moves, with his subordinates and allies exercising ity over the better known trade paths. Thus by 1879 turned his warriors to the conquest of the areas interver tween Unyanyembe and Ujiji. From May until October Mirambo and his allies, with a force estimated by one at 4000 men, were active in Uvinza and Uha. The c were successful; Mirambo secured many prisoners ir releasing them only after they were ransomed by thei

with ivory. According to Mirambo the Uha venture had another
motive than mere conquest; he claimed that a Ha ruler had been
extracting too much in passage tolls from his caravans, but this
is a moot point. The strategy followed against the Ha offers a
good illustration of the nature of Mirambo's military tactics.
He marched from Urambo in an opposite direction from his goal,
then later changing direction when unobserved by the enemy to
return and take the Ha by surprise. To demonstrate the pressure
maintained on Mirambo by his martial followers, despite the
active campaigning already accomplished in 1879, 1200 of his
warriors from the different areas of Urambo came to their leader
in November to request a new campaign since "they were tired
of inactivity."

The clamoring soldiers had not long to wait for additional
action; in February 1880 Mirambo returned to campaigning in
Usukuma, supported by one of the most prominent of his Nyamwezi subordinates, Ntinginya of Usongo, a state to the north of
Urambo. It appears that certain Arabs had been attempting to
bypass Ntinginya whose duty it was to control one section of the
route to Lake Victoria. Thus a wider swath of territory had to
be brought under submission to Mirambo to prevent the attempted evasions. Mirambo was back in his capital in March,
but at the end of May he was off again on the campaign which
led to the deaths of Carter and Cadenhead. The Urambo *ntemi*
led a force of 7000 warriors, so Southon claimed, besides carrying
along a cannon and 2500 pounds of gunpowder, on this expedition originally aimed for the Ugala River regions. It was once
more claimed by Mirambo that a local ruler, Ntakama, was interfering with the caravan trade of his subjects. The counsels of
Kirk, explained to Mirambo by Southon, against extensive campaigning must have prompted the war leader to advance this
weak defense of his normal activity. There were also reports that
during this foray Mirambo would deal with his old enemies, the
Nyamwezi of Ugunda, since they had been drawing support from
Isike, the *ntemi* of Unyanyembe. But the campaign closed with
the Mpimbwe affair, with Mirambo hurrying back to Urambo to
attempt to extricate himself from his unexpected difficulties.
Fortunately Southon was present with Mirambo in August to

record one of the usual events which followed a successful campaign. Mirambo's actions here offer significant comment on his perception of the campaign ending at Mpimbwe: it had been successful, he had defeated his enemies, and there was no reason to let what he hoped was merely a temporary dissatisfaction on the part of the British interfere with the traditional proceedings of the Urambo war state. Mirambo then presided over the ceremoney of dividing the slave booty, mostly of women and young children, returned to his capital by the victorious army. Any warrior having taken one or more prisoners in the course of the expedition brought them before his *ntemi,* with Mirambo taking about one-half of those presented. If an individual warrior had demonstrated conspicuous bravery, Mirambo allowed him to retain his entire booty. And for those who had performed bravely, without being successful in taking any slaves, Mirambo rewarded them from the slaves given to him. When the ceremony was over Mirambo had left for himself only about twenty slaves. By this period of Mirambo's career, such distribution of slaves was a vital proceeding. With his subjects virtually always busy at the tasks of war, slaves had to be utilized extensively to ensure the agricultural prosperity of Urambo.

The campaigns of 1881 had two principal goals. In April, Mirambo undertook activities in the regions between Urambo and Lake Victoria. This time victories brought Mirambo's influence right to the shores of the lake. The significant event of the campaign was the triumph over the chief of Msalala on Smith Sound; he was killed in the fighting and the new leader was dependent upon Mirambo. Mirambo's check with Kirk had not deprived him of the ability to continue devising ambitious schemes; the Urambo *ntemi,* now with an outlet on Lake Victoria, sought to open friendly relations with Mutesa of Buganda. The Nyamwezi ruler wanted Mutesa to use his numerous warriors to conquer the peoples on the western shore of Lake Victoria, thus opening up a safe trade route between Urambo and Buganda. In July it was reported that Mutesa had agreed to move against one of the hostile Zinza chiefdoms on the proposed route. But although Mutesa was willing to accept Mirambo's presents, all negotiations between the two rulers proved fruitless; Mirambo and Mutesa never concluded an effective alliance. Even without the alliance, however, this northern campaign had been successful. At one ceremony in Urambo in April, Mirambo had distributed among his warriors a war booty of 3000 cattle.

Mirambo had too many warriors to use only in campaigns under his personal direction; there were always smaller expeditions directed by subordinates ravaging selected areas while their leader was busy elsewhere. Early in 1881 such an independent expedition was actively raiding in the regions south of Unyanyembe, especially around the Ugala River. There was also fighting near Unyanyembe where Mirambo's men were defeated at a village friendly to Isike. Richard Böhm, a member of the German International African Association settled in Ugunda, traveled through the Ugala area in March, finding wide devastation, with the inhabitants much in fear of the return of Mirambo's men. The fear was justified. In October, Mirambo led his army against his erstwhile ally of the Mpimbwe battle, Simba of Usawila. One reason for this campaign, besides the prosaic one of removing a powerful rival, was suggested by Adolphe Burdo of the International African Association—that Mirambo blamed Simba for the Carter and Cadenhead affair since he had not informed the Urambo *ntemi* that Kasogera had two Britons in his village. One observer, the missionary Dr. Baxter, had in fact learned from one of Carter's followers that Simba, when learning before the attack of the presence of the two Europeans, had said to his men, "Did I not tell him [Carter] when he wished to return to the coast to pass my way and now he is returning by another route, fight him."[1] Mirambo may have had some such reason for being dissatisfied with Simba over Mpimbwe, but this author does not believe that the principal responsibility for the affair can be removed from Mirambo. In the contest with Simba, Mirambo secured an easy victory, despite his rival's impressively fortified village—Simba's palisades enclosed a three-quarter-mile area—by disguising some of his men as refugees fleeing his advance. They were admitted inside Simba's fortifications, later successfully opening an entry for their leader's warriors. Simba

[1] Baxter to Church Missionary Society, Aug. 9, 1880, in Lister to Kirk, Sept. 24, 1880, Q-23, ZA.

escaped the defeat, but his once powerful position of influence on the route to Lake Tanganyika was no more. Mirambo at once had constructed a new center to secure continued domination of the peoples along the route. All coming that way henceforth would be required to meet Mirambo's demands.

DIFFICULTIES WITH THE INTERNATIONAL AFRICAN ASSOCIATION

The campaign against Simba brought Mirambo once more into a period of strained relationships with the Belgian members of the International African Association. His *ruga-ruga* waged war in the regions neighboring Karema; during October 1881 a large band of his followers conquered all the villages to within a day's march of the station. By the end of the year rumors were circulating that Mirambo planned to seize the station at Karema, whose possession by the association he had never recognized. And if Mirambo's claims to authority had been somewhat vague in the past, he now could claim it by conquest, through the defeat of the elephant hunter Matumera with whom Cambier had dealt for the possession of the territory. Matumera had been a dependent ally of Simba of Usawila, meeting defeat along with his master. According to rumors there was also a new and possibly more convincing reason for action by Mirambo at this time: there were supposedly large quantities of gunpowder stored at Karema, supplies which could help alleviate the effects of the shortage to Mirambo's warriors caused by the Sultan of Zanzibar's coastal gunpowder blockade. Additional pressure on the Belgians came when Mirambo's commanders—he was not then leading his men—demanded tribute from Captain Ramaeckers, Karema's commander. The Belgian officer refused the demand, informing the *ruga-ruga* leaders that they had no credentials with them to prove they were actually acting in Mirambo's behalf. The Nyamwezi warriors accepted the refusal without a hostile reaction, but clearly the International African Association could not rest easy over the potential danger facing their most important East African station. Ramaeckers, who considered that the Africans around Karema supported the association's rule, and not Mirambo's, began perfecting the defenses of his isolated post.

Then, to heighten the uncertainty, Ramaeckers, one of the most able of the Belgians in East Africa, died of dysentery in February 1882.

The directors of the association had originally planned to have Ramaeckers visit Urambo to talk over their troubled relations with its *ntemi,* thereby demonstrating their readiness to let the Carter and Cadenhead affair pass without reprisal. It was hoped that during the talks all would be smoothed over and that Ramaeckers would find it possible to enter into an informal agreement with Southon so that both could work to keep relations between Mirambo and the Belgians stable for the future. The association, of course, had little alternative since they lacked the military force to take offensive measures against Mirambo. In face of the unexpected news of Ramaecker's death, with rumors crowding around about the fate of Karema, another Belgian officer, then detained in Unyanyembe, decided to act upon his own initiative in the hope of stabilizing the dangerous situation. Lieutenant Jerome Becker, a talented, impulsive young man, later to become well known as one of the closest European friends of the Arab leader, Tippu Tip, as well as for his gripping and informative account of his experiences in East Africa, *La Vie en Afrique,* hurried in February 1882 to talk with Mirambo at his new capital, Ikonongo. Mirambo completely charmed his guest, making an even more favorable impression upon Becker than he did upon other visitors to Urambo. In the hours of their long discussions, ranging freely over the entire course of Mirambo's career, Becker finally introduced the topic of the recent threats to Karema. Mirambo claimed that he was entirely ignorant of the reported activities of his followers around the Belgian station —which could have been true. He explained that since no Belgians had visited Urambo from the time of Cambier's hurried departure, his men might have considered them enemies. Nevertheless Mirambo at once promised to punish the guilty leader of the implicated band of *ruga-ruga* (later it was reported that the unlucky warrior-leader responsible for worrying Ramaeckers had actually been executed). Then, after expressing his strong dissatisfaction with the association's establishment at Karema and with Cambier's behavior before and after arriving at the station, Mirambo generously agreed to permit the Belgians to continue their occupation of the Lake Tanganyika establishment. Moreover they could do so without paying any tribute to him as its sovereign. When Becker, stirred by his sudden apparent success, pressed to secure this statement in written form, Mirambo haughtily refused, stating that his spoken word was enough for any agreement. Becker, perforce, accepted this reply, leaving Mirambo with a feeling of intense satisfaction about the result of his unauthorized mission. When he reached Karema to take command, Becker received two of Mirambo's delegates sent by their master to make the Belgian a formal delegation of the authority to occupy the station.

The young officer-turned-diplomat had forgotten, or had never understood, one important matter in these discussions at Urambo leading to the agreement concerning Karema. By accepting Mirambo's seemingly gracious decision, Becker had acknowledged that the African leader actually did possess a genuine claim to the sovereignty of the Karema region, something which the Brussels-based directors of the International African Association had never admitted. M. Strauch of the association had in fact made this very point in a February 1882 letter to Ramaeckers authorizing that unfortunate officer's visit to Mirambo; he was to make the visit an informal one, merely stopping as any traveler to talk with Mirambo as he marched on his return to Zanzibar. Again in April, not knowing of Ramaecker's death, Strauch wrote once more, this time approving the Karema commander's refusal to allow Becker to visit Mirambo; the directors of the association concurred in the opinion that he did not possess the talents necessary for negotiations concerning delicate diplomatic affairs. But however Strauch's displeasure was expressed upon hearing of Becker's visit, there was little sense by that time in any alternative response. All involved in the work of the association simply avoided any overt recognition of Mirambo's supposed sovereignty over Karema; Lieutenant Emile Storms, the station's last Belgian commander, received strict orders against any repetition of Becker's proceedings. And since no more bands of the Nyamwezi ruler menaced the Lake Tanganyika station, Urambo-International African Association relations remained untroubled during the

remaining few years of Mirambo's life. There was one brief moment of worry when Mirambo's warriors besieged and overran a
village near Karema in 1884, but no moves were subsequently
made endangering Karema. The work of the association in East
Africa did not long survive Mirambo; increasingly more interested in the Congo River regions, and concerned with Germany's
moving into East Africa, Leopold evacuated his Lake Tanganyika stations in 1885.

However important Becker's visit was to the International
African Association, it was merely of passing interest to Mirambo,
who probably had never planned any hostile moves against
Karema. The Mpimbwe affair had caused him enough trouble
with the representatives of the European world located in Zanzibar without inciting their further displeasure for the gain of
an unprosperous locality situated far from the important trading
routes of eastern Africa. Instead, during 1882, Mirambo continued his usual campaigning, reaffirming his authority to the
east of the Malagarazi River, this river probably being the effective western limit of his territory toward Lake Tanganyika on
the main route from Unyanyembe. He also again led his warriors to Msalala near Lake Victoria. While there Mirambo seized
upon the opportune presence of a Church Missionary Society
group to demonstrate his continued friendship for Europeans
by ordering the new ruler of Msalala to allow the interested missionaries to proceed as they liked throughout his territory.

MIRAMBO AND SOUTHON

Meanwhile, all during this busy period, Mirambo continued to
remain on the best of terms with Ebenezer Southon of the London Missionary Society. Southon's career as a political adviser
had received a definite setback from the Zanzibar reactions to
the deaths of Carter and Cadenhead, but his purely missionary
endeavors were not at all adversely affected. The medical missionary undertook more extensive work among Mirambo's peoples than his cautious directors thought wise. Southon had
established a hospital in Urambo despite the clear orders of his
superiors not to do so since it would too much draw him away

from missionary tasks that they considered more important. Southon angrily informed the London bureaucrats that the hospital had already been in existence for a year before he had received their opposing statement, and that his treatment of Urambo residents was a great aid to his regular mission work. He further answered with asperity that he did not require any London Missionary Society funds for the hospital's functioning because he ran the hospital on donations from private individuals not connected with his missionary organization. The directors wisely let the matter drop, realizing that Southon, despite his obstinate disobedience, was one of their most effective representatives in Africa; the hospital remained in operation. As for the African inhabitants of Urambo, this decision was all to the good. They yet followed the attitude of their *ntemi*, showing little interest in Southon's efforts in proselytizing or in Christian education, but his medical skills were another matter; in the year ending in December 1880 Southon had treated over 1600 Nyamwezi. Mirambo himself profited from a second operation for the removal of another troublesome tumor from his arm.

Southon's isolation from sustained European contacts ended with the arrival of a missionary reinforcement, David Williams, in September 1880. Not long after the London Missionary Society men in East Africa, meeting as the local governing board of the mission, recommended the creation of additional stations among the Nyamwezi. They were doubtless stimulated by the ebullient reports of the new man, Williams; he praised the Nyamwezi as being "more intelligent, courageous, enterprizing and industrious" than any other African people he had encountered on his journey inland. Shortage of missionary recruits blocked these optimistic plans; then in November 1881 Williams died in Urambo from sunstroke. His year of life with Mirambo had made little impact upon the work of the mission since he had unfortunately not proved a congenial partner for Southon. The latter's only other British missionary companion was Walter Hutley, an experienced lay missionary from Ujiji, one of the original Lake Tanganyika group, who visited Mirambo's center in 1881 to recuperate from fever and the other harmful effects of his long stay in the lake environment. Hutley, impressed with the mission's work among the Nyamwezi, remained past his scheduled time of return. Southon, to his great displeasure, had also been ordered to remove to the lake for a change of scenery during this period, but the loss of Williams and the departure of Hutley through necessity allowed the medical missionary to remain at his beloved station. From then on, Southon worked diligently and efficiently to perfect the mission establishment which Jerome Becker described during his visit to Mirambo as "an Eden in miniature." One other activity of the missionary, of significance to the future, occurred in 1882 when Southon had printed by the Universities' Mission press in Zanzibar a few copies of a primer he had written in the Nyamwezi language for the furtherance of his educational work.

Mirambo, who had already learned much of the intricacies of European rivalries from the men of many nationalities who had visited Urambo, learned from Southon of their religious rivalries as well. The Roman Catholic White Fathers, a French organization directed from Algiers by the brilliant and determined Cardinal Lavigerie, had in 1878 followed their Protestant counterparts to East Africa. Busily engaged elsewhere, especially in the areas around Lake Tanganyika and Lake Victoria, the Catholic order had not had time, nor men, to spare for the Nyamwezi. However, members of the society had visited Mirambo as early as 1879, and they were as interested as the Protestants in establishing a mission among his vigorous people. The White Fathers did found a station in Unyanyembe in 1881, while several passing priests had discussions with Mirambo about founding another station within his dominions. When, in 1881, Southon learned that some White Fathers were experiencing difficulties on their journey to Buganda and consequently might visit Mirambo, he emphatically warned the Nyamwezi leader that such men were the "avowed enemies" of Protestant groups like the London Missionary Society. He secured from Mirambo the promise that only British missionaries could settle on his lands. But the Roman Catholics were unable to visit Mirambo thus saving Urambo from mission rivalry. Southon, a tolerant man in most of his actions, explained his attitude to Mirambo in these harsh words: "It has ever been my determination to resist any attempt on the part of the Jesuits [i.e. the White Fathers] to come to Urambo. I should deem it my duty to God to hold aloof from them if they intended to settle in my sphere of labour. Here let me say that I must express surprize that Members of Christian Societies should so fraternize with the Jesuits in this country as they do. . . . These avowed enemies of the Cross of Christ should everywhere be treated as such." In fairness to the London Missionary Society officials, it is necessary to add that they scarcely shared Southon's extreme views; Foreign Secretary Ralph W. Thomson answered Southon's intemperate outburst by stating, "I confess I had rather see the work done by them than that nothing should be done."

Southon had one function above all to fulfill for Mirambo, that of being his link with the British in Zanzibar. He remained useful since Mirambo continued attempting to win back the favor of John Kirk. During 1882 Mirambo was especially dissatisfied with his lack of progress to that goal. There were difficulties then for Mirambo with Isike, *ntemi* of Unyanyembe, who was firmly under Arab influence. And, above all, the continuing gunpowder blockade imposed by the Sultan of Zanzibar was proving a bothersome obstacle during Mirambo's campaigns; Africans in opposition to the Urambo leader had no difficulty in gaining gunpowder. Thus in March 1882 Mirambo dictated what he hoped would prove a convincing letter for Colonel S. B. Miles, Kirk's temporary replacement in Zanzibar. "Tell the British Consul," Southon wrote for Mirambo, "I only ask a more rigid investigation of my affairs in connection with other tribes around me and in the interest of trade I would respectfully ask that he would send some responsible agent from his office to dictate the line of policy I should pursue towards others at the same time giving me his help and support in carrying these out. I am aware that the constant fighting I am compelled to do is displeasing to him, but I am really trying to reduce this to a minimum and I hope soon to live at peace with all around me." Mirambo went on to complain that he had recently dispatched one of his relatives to Zanzibar to attempt settling all the outstanding differences between himself and the British and Zanzibari authorities. But once there the ambassador reported to

Mirambo that both the sultan and Miles refused him a hearing. Even more, his present to Barghash was refused. Was this all true, Mirambo asked? And apparently fearing it was, Mirambo continued attempting to justify his usefulness to Zanzibar and Briton alike, concluding that "I wish to open it [my country] up, to learn of Europeans, to trade honestly with all and to cultivate peaceful relationships with my neighbors." Southon joined his already known approval to these sentiments by affirming that he believed Mirambo to be sincere in all his statements. Miles left the matter for Kirk's resolution; he was not in any case sympathetic to Southon. Edward Hore reported that the official had once had the missionary's goods searched in Zanzibar to determine if they concealed gunpowder destined for Mirambo. The London officials of Southon's society attempted to add their support to the words of Mirambo meant for John Kirk, inviting the British diplomat, then on leave in Great Britain, to a meeting of the London Missionary Society's board of directors. "But he gave us a very polite rebuff," lamented Foreign Secretary Thomson, "by saying that he did not see that anything could be gained by such an interview. And he is evidently thoroughly prejudiced against Mirambo." Despite the rebuff, Mirambo refused to give up hope. When he aided a Church Missionary Society expedition to reach Lake Victoria in September 1882, he directed the lay missionary, Charles Stokes, "Now . . . you will write and tell your big people that Mirambo the robber is changed, and he has now a peaceful country." The message evoked as little response as the previous ones; 1882 closed with no change in Kirk's attitude to Mirambo.

Before this last letter was written, Ebenezer Southon's East African career had ended. In July 1882 the medical missionary left on a hunting expedition designed to stimulate his indifferent health. Tragedy struck without warning; Southon was accidentally shot in the elbow by an African companion carrying his rifle. Suffering great pain, and unable to treat himself adequately, Southon sought outside assistance. The only nearby European, Arthur Copplestone of the Church Missionary Society, hurried to Urambo from Uyui ready to do what he could. He was appalled to learn that Southon considered it necessary for part of his arm to be amputated because of spreading gangrene. Steeling himself to perform the necessary operation, Copplestone removed the arm above the elbow, guided by the advice Southon could give him. But the harassed Copplestone had to admit when his first surgical venture was completed, "a few important items was [sic] not shown to me." Southon remained in extreme pain, with open bone and nerve ends, and it was distressingly obvious that another operation was required. Copplestone sent to the German International Association based in Ugunda for Dr. Richard Böhm, hoping that he was a medical doctor. He was not. Thus Copplestone, with the assistance of the German naturalist, performed a second harrowing operation. The result was no more successful, and after days of great suffering during which Southon may have inadvertently taken some harmful medicine, the Urambo missionary died on July 26, 1882.

With this unexpected death, Mirambo lost his most valuable European adviser, his closest European friend. Southon had come to Urambo to work for the good, as he envisaged it, of its Nyamwezi inhabitants. His efforts to spread Christianity, as far as we can judge, met with little response either from Mirambo or his followers. But Southon was a compassionate man, devoted to aiding the physical well-being of the people he worked among, always hoping, without allowing his failures in spreading Christian doctrine to embitter his relations with Africans, that the spiritual goals he worked for would in the long run triumph. One typical example of Southon's reactions to Africa and Africans is given in an amusing episode reported by the Belgian officer, Emile Storms. Mirambo had forbidden the discharge of firearms around his center unless the action was necessary for killing a lion or repulsing an enemy. Southon, while out on one of his frequent hunting expeditions, ignored the dictum; suddenly he was seized by some of Mirambo's *ruga-ruga* who struck him with sticks while they took him as a prisoner to a nearby village. Recognized by the African inhabitants, Southon was freed, with Mirambo later apologizing for the treatment by sending the missionary a gift of cattle.[2] Southon never mentioned

2 Storms, Mpala Journal, Dec. 9, 1884, Storm Papers, Musée de l'Afrique Centrale, Tervuren.

the episode in his writings, nor did he use it as many Europeans might have done, to win advantage for his position by treating the affair as a serious affront to European dignity. Apparently Southon decided that since he had violated the laws of Urambo, the state where he labored of his own free will, he would suffer the consequences with a good grace.

And during his life in Urambo, Southon provided Mirambo with a vital link to the world outside the plateau land of the Nyamwezi. Whatever Mirambo learned of the European way of life, he learned mostly from Southon. The missionary's role is obvious enough from his sustained correspondence with Kirk. Southon never doubted Mirambo's good faith as a man; his re-action to the deaths of Carter and Cadenhead clearly indicated his trust in the character of the Nyamwezi leader. In Ebenezer Southon of the London Missionary Society, the missionary world of the nineteenth century had one of its finest representatives. By twentieth-century standards he was a religious bigot, but by the standards of his own time his prejudices were understand-able, if not laudable. Finally, to Mirambo, Southon's loss had to be important; he would not be replaced in the valuable counsel he had given to the African ruler who was attempting the difficult task of understanding the European world which had so suddenly thrust itself into the political life of inland East Africa.

The London Missionary Society reacted immediately to the news of Southon's death with the dispatch of new missionaries to replace their departed representative. W. C. Willoughby and Thomas F. Shaw arrived in Urambo in November 1882 to carry on the society's work. Whatever the success of their Christian endeavors, which seemed as little noteworthy at first as those of Southon, they did not fill the political void left by the loss of their predecessor. Willoughby is remembered for little except his useful brief biographical study of Mirambo and for his con-tinuation of Southon's anti-Roman Catholic bias. When in 1883 the White Fathers renewed their discussions with Mirambo concerning a station in his territory, Willoughby felt compelled to protest to the Urambo *ntemi* that "these men were not our brothers, but the enemies of our work; that our objects were entirely distinct; that we wanted to educate the people but that it was their policy to keep them ignorant." Mirambo was told that he must choose between the two groups of missionaries, and Willoughby proudly reported that he chose the London Missionary Society. But the influence of the Protestant missionaries was no longer the same; it was an indication of the difference in value Mirambo attributed to his residents since despite his promise to Willoughby he actually had given the French priests permission to settle. He allowed the White Fathers, when they were ready in April 1884, to establish a mission in his dominions.

Thomas Shaw was an individual more after the pattern of Southon, although the changed conditions in Urambo, brought about by Mirambo's declining health, did not allow him to exercise Southon's influence. Shaw remained in Urambo as the soul of the London Missionary Society endeavor until 1895, providing valuable, if often ignored, counsel to Mirambo's weak successors. He came to Urambo with high recommendations. Shaw's pastor well described the man in his evaluation letter to the London Missionary Society: "He has rare powers of observation; discerns men and things in a way few young men are able to do; has a retentive memory for facts and thought rather than for words; is peculiarly apt at the study of languages. . . . I consider . . . he is able to meet difficulties such as any missionary may have to encounter." The evaluation was correct enough, but the time left for Mirambo was limited and Shaw performed his services for Urambo, which were considerable (including the valuable legacy of his letters and journals), mostly when that African state was in full decline.

MIRAMBO AND TIPPU TIP

Yet, while the importance of Mirambo's European advisers declined after the death of Southon, the resourceful ruler of Urambo did not give up in his endeavors to moderate the unfavorable political and economic stances of the Arabs of Unyanyembe and the authorities of Zanzibar. A new opportunity for Mirambo to act came during 1882, made possible by the return to Zanzibar of the most powerful Arab of the eastern Congo region, Manyema. Tippu Tip, the sobriquet for the Zanzibar-born Arab, Hamid bin Muhammed el Murjebi, had by 1882 reached the highest peak of success possible for a subject of the rulers of Zanzibar. While most of the Arabs of Zanzibar who were active in the African interior had to remain content with a role of more or less influence over an African ruler, or a series of rulers, as we have observed with the Arabs among the Nyamwezi of Unyanyembe, Tippu Tip, along with several other noteworthy former inhabitants of Zanzibar and the East African coast, had established an extensive personal empire among the politically fragmented peoples of Manyema. Based in the Congo River centers of Nyangwe and Kasongo, plus several lesser towns, these Arabs exercised direct political authority over the militarily weak inhabitants of the region. The result was the winning of truly prodigious amounts of ivory—Manyema was one of the richest ivory-producing areas of all Africa—along with an abundant harvest of slaves. The latter were valued both as followers for the Arabs and for their profitable sale along the trade routes to the East African coast. Very few reached the coast, however, until later years. This rape of a virtually helpless African population began at a relatively late date, in the 1860's, although even in the early 1870's the region was unknown enough for the usually informed John Kirk to write with puzzlement from Zanzibar that he could learn practically nothing about Manyema except "it is an ivory-country, visited by the Ujiji traders," who, Kirk added, "seldom came to the coast."[3]

Tippu Tip first arrived in Manyema around 1860, using his masterly organizing abilities to make himself the foremost, although not the absolutely dominant, Arab ruler of the region. After completing an extensive stay, having collected a massive haul of ivory, about 2000 tusks, Tippu Tip set forth with a caravan of 3000 men (all this information according to the report of eye-witness Jerome Becker), one of the largest groups ever to pass along the Manyema-Ujiji-Unyanyembe route to Zanzibar. Clearly this outstanding individual, described later by an Irish

[3] Kirk to Rawlinson, Jan. 15, 1872, *Proceedings of the Royal Geographical Society*, 16 (1871-72), 227.

companion of Henry Stanley, Dr. Thomas Parke, as "standing . . . nearly six feet, with bright intelligent black eyes, and displaying manners of imperial dignity and courtesy,"[4] was a man whose influence Mirambo could hope to benefit from if he could convince the Arab to plead his case before the sultan.

And according to local traditions, Mirambo had a special relationship with Tippu Tip which contributed to this hope. It was said that Tippu Tip's grandfather, Juma bin Rajab, the father of Muhammad bin Juma whose activities against Msabila of Unyanyembe have previously been noted, had established Mirambo's grandfather as the ruling chief of Uyowa. The circumstances and validity of the tradition are unclear, but if Juma bin Rajab actually did play the role of chiefmaker, the subsequent relations between Mirambo and Tippu Tip become yet more understandable. But even if there were no special relationships between the grandfathers of the Arab and Nyamwezi leaders, there were obvious advantages for both Mirambo and Tippu Tip in reaching agreement. Mirambo needed an influential supporter to plead his case with Sultan Barghash; this was particularly true during 1882 when there were indications that the Arabs of Unyanyembe, perhaps with Barghash's support, were preparing for war against Urambo. And Tippu Tip, with his large and vulnerable caravan, needed assurance that he could pass the regions subject to Mirambo's *ruga-ruga* in peace.

Tippu Tip's requirements were the more acute. His expedition had become involved in significant hostilities while crossing the territories of the Vinza to the west of the Malagarasi River. One explanation of the difficulties was that a Vinza tribesman had committed a minor theft from Tippu Tip's caravan; the Arab reprisals had then led to more general fighting. Whatever the cause, the fighting was intense, with Tippu Tip hurrying his ivory-laden followers into the Unyanyembe capital, in September 1881, where he could secure adequate supplies of gunpowder to allow his military escort to return to chastise the Vinza. But Tippu Tip had one development to fear. The Vinza, meantime,

4 T. H. Parke, *My Personal Experiences in Equatorial Africa* (London, 1891), 18.

under Chief Kasanura, had sent to Mirambo to request his aid
against their Arab enemies. Since the Nyamwezi rivals of Unyanyembe and Urambo usually knew what was occurring in each
other's territories, the potential danger to Tippu Tip must have
been obvious enough for him to make an agreement with Mirambo.

While Tippu Tip pondered his alternatives, the Arabs of
Unyanyembe tried to gain the powerful leader's support against
Mirambo. Relations between Urambo and Unyanyembe had
become very troubled by 1882—there had been minor hostilities
at the beginning of the year—and there were substantial fears
among the Arab leaders that the widespread disorders of the early
1870's might recur. But Tippu Tip, whose economic interests in
the Congo dwarfed those of the Arabs around Unyanyembe, had
no intention of letting himself be drawn into a struggle, from
which he had nothing to gain. Any sentimental ties the great
Arab had with Unyanyembe's Arab community had probably
ended with the death of his father, Muhammad bin Juma, in
January 1882. Thus according to Tippu Tip's later version of
events, when Mirambo sent ambassadors to him, via the intermediary of Muhammad bin Juma, bearing gifts of ivory and
slave girls, and of more interest, the offer of a peaceful passage
through his territories, the Arab leader did not hesitate to seize
upon the proferred friendship despite the unhappy rumblings
of his Muslim compatriots in Unyanyembe. Tippu Tip immediately dispatched six of his trusted followers to visit Urambo;
although Mirambo was then absent on his victorious campaign
against Simba of Usawila, the visitors were treated royally by
Mpandashalo, Mirambo's brother, who was one of his most
trusted military commanders. On their return to Tippu Tip, the
Arab leader, encouraged by his men's accounts of their visit, and
especially at the news of Mirambo's refusal to aid the Vinza
against him, responded to a new invitation from the Urambo
ntemi by sending his son, Sefu bin Muhammed, one of his most
trusted subordinates, to Urambo. The Unyanyembe Arabs were
most upset at this turn of events, but Tippu Tip, who had already heard from them a whole series of unfounded rumors about
the dangers he faced from Mirambo, refused to believe any of

the alarmist warnings they advanced about the perils his son faced by traveling to Urambo.

When Sefu bin Muhammed reached Urambo, Mirambo received the visitor in his most affable style. We have a third-party report of some of the proceedings from another visitor then with Mirambo, the able German army officer and explorer Hermann Wissmann, who was completing his successful trans-African trip from the Atlantic coast to Zanzibar via the Arab establishments along the Congo River. Wissmann's observations modify somewhat the account of the Arab-Mirambo transactions as recorded in Tippu Tip's autobiography. The German explorer reported that Sefu bin Muhammed was the suppliant, actively seeking to gain if not the support of Mirambo for his father's passing caravan, at least his passive acquiescence in letting it proceed through his territories. Tippu Tip's account placed the desire for reaching an agreement with Mirambo. There was truth in both views; the Arab and African leaders needed each other's support. They proved this by speedily concluding an arrangement whereby Tippu Tip's expedition was allowed to pass in peace, while the Arab promised to reciprocate by using his considerable influence in Zanzibar with Sultan Barghash to secure for Mirambo the position he sought in the interior. But before the conclusion of this agreement the Unyanyembe Arabs made one final attempt to incite hostilities between Mirambo and Tippu Tip. Ten Nyamwezi, clothed as if they had just returned from the East African coast, hurried into Mirambo's capital to warn the *ntemi* that a large force, sent by the Sultan of Zanzibar, was en route to take offensive action against him. Mirambo was not to be duped; he realized that the men came from his enemies and thus kept all in Urambo calm until the news of the threatening expedition was learned to be untrue. Wissmann later claimed that he had intervened to protect Tippu Tip's son from these intrigues, but although the German certainly did attempt to do what he could, his aid was not at all needed by the diligently watchful Mirambo. Sefu bin Muhammed then returned to Unyanyembe—he had of course been a potentially useful hostage for Mirambo until the news of the coast expedition proved false—with the good news for his father.

With Mirambo's passive approval, Tippu Tip and his many
followers reached Zanzibar without any untoward incident. It is
not known how forcefully, if at all, the Arab leader argued Mirambo's case with his sovereign, but it seems likely that he did
not press the African ruler's case before Barghash with any vigor.
In view of the Zanzibar attitude to Mirambo, which he must
have soon discovered, it would have been only a wasted effort.
And however he acted, no change in attitude occurred in Zanzibar toward the Nyamwezi leader. John Kirk stuck steadfastly to
his revised policy of using Zanzibar as the main stabilizer of the
interior, even approaching Tippu Tip to determine if he might
play a major role along the Nyamwezi caravan route. Kirk did
so because there was then a prime opportunity for him to take
advantage of a change in the leadership of the Arab community
in Unyanyembe. The sultan's *liwali*, Abdulla bin Nasibu, had
been recalled to Zanzibar in 1881; what is more surprising the
liwali actually heeded the distant sultan's order to return. The
supposed reason for the recall was Abdulla bin Nasibu's mistreat-
ment of Emile Sergère, a European trader at Unyanyembe. This
Frenchman, who had been employed by the Marseilles firm of
Roux de Fraissinet, following the example of Philippe Broyon
had decided to open a center for the purchase of ivory in Unyanyembe. He also had extensive plans, in partnership with the
rising Indian merchant, Sewa Haji Paru (who would during the
German period in East Africa become one of the region's richest
men), to open caravan supply bases at Unyanyembe and elsewhere on the routes between the far interior and the coast. At
these various centers, well stocked with all the necessities of
travel, caravan leaders could arrange for purchases on letters of
credit for Zanzibar, and consequently much of the trouble of
inland African travel would have been dissipated.

The Arabs were aroused at this direct challenge to their commercial position. When it was learned that Sergère was negotiating with Mirambo, allegedly for the sale of firearms and gunpowder, the Arabs combined with Mirambo's Nyamwezi rival,
Isike of Unyanyembe, to force Sergère to flee to the coast under
threat of losing his life. His claimed connection with Mirambo
appears true since Kirk wrote that he knew of an agreement, and

that Sergère was bringing some field pieces inland for Mirambo. With his hurried departure the harassed French trader had to abandon most of his possessions to the Arabs and Africans of Unyanyembe. Sergère's case was taken up in Zanzibar by the French consul. Either the pressure from this European official, or the fact that Abdulla bin Nasibu was heavily in debt to the Indian merchants of Zanzibar, apparently caused Sultan Barghash to order his Arab subordinate's return. The debts were real enough; in 1879 the Church Missionary Society member J. T. Last had reported that Abdulla bin Nasibu was so much in debt that he did not "dare show his face at the [Zanzibar] court."[5] The owing of heavy debts to the Indians of Zanzibar was not an unusual phenomenon. The Belgian Emile Storms said that Tippu Tip, during his 1881-82 stay in Unyanyembe, had sold much of his ivory at that center since he knew much of what he carried would have been immediately held for his Indian creditors on his return to his home island.[6] Perhaps Sergère's business associate, Sewa Haji Paru, sharing in the losses caused by the *liwali*'s expulsion of Sergère from Unyanyembe, was an important stimulant in rousing the Indian creditors of Abdulla bin Nasibu to exert pressure upon Barghash. There also might have been political implications in the recall since Last's colleague Alexander Mackay placed Abdulla bin Nasibu among the members of a faction, led by Barghash's brother Ali bin Said, which had recently engaged in intrigues designed to overthrow the ruler of Zanzibar. Whatever the reason for the summons to Zanzibar, Abdulla bin Nasibu answered the call, perhaps motivated by reported threats from the sultan to seize his family's property in Zanzibar, or to attack him in Unyanyembe—so said the German explorer Paul Reichard. When the *liwali* reached Zanzibar he was immediately imprisoned. He never regained his position in Unyanyembe. In 1882 Abdulla bin Nasibu, Mirambo's oldest and most determined Arab enemy, died; some claimed that he was poisoned through the orders of Barghash as he was attempting to return to Unyanyembe.

5 Last to Wright, March 5, 1879, C.A6/014, CMS.
6 Storms, Journal, 1882, Storms Papers.

Thus there was no *liwali* in Unyanyembe, even though Shaykh
bin Nasibu initially acted unofficially to fill the position during
his brother's absence. But he too died in 1882, again it was said
through poison administered on Barghash's orders. It was therefore proposed, perhaps through the Customs Master of Zanzibar,
to Tippu Tip that he accepted the appointment of *liwali* at
Unyanyembe. This was not a very realistic offer to the powerful
Arab magnate of the much more important Congo ivory regions,
and Tippu Tip never seriously considered accepting the position.
But there was a related suggestion that Tippu Tip's brother,
Muhammed Masudi, take the office. This alternative also was not
accepted. Either of the men would have made a useful ally for
Mirambo because of the good relationships established during
Tippu Tip's return journey to Zanzibar. Conversely, Isike of
Unyanyembe was almost in panic at the early rumors that these
friends of Mirambo might arrive in his capital. In the end Barghash took no action at all; no successor to Abdulla bin Nasibu
was ever appointed by the Arab ruler. The Arab community of
Unyanyembe, left without an effective leader, and with many of
its members leaving to seek the wealth of Manyema, henceforth
went into serious decline. A growing factionalism among the remaining Arabs further contributed to their weakness. There no
longer would be any serious threats to Mirambo from this source,
although with the decline of the Arabs the formerly subservient
ntemi, Isike, began a career of his own which eventually developed into a serious challenge to his Nyamwezi rival in Urambo.

With his business successfully accomplished in Zanzibar, and
all political offers declined, Tippu Tip left the island in early
1883 to return to his Congo dominions. Lacking sufficient men
for his many loads, the Arab leader sent ahead to Urambo requesting aid; Mirambo at once dispatched a large contingent of
Nyamwezi carriers to help Tippu Tip on his way. Thus encouraged Tippu Tip, losing his earlier caution, decided to visit
Urambo. We have only a few words from Tippu Tip to describe
this memorable meeting between two of east central Africa's great
men. The Arab was extremely pleased with his reception, reporting "Great honor was accorded to me and a great friendship was
established." Mirambo utilized the meeting to renew his requests

for Tippu Tip's intervention on his behalf in Zanzibar, and the
Arab once again promised to do what he could. Obviously, since
he was returning to the Congo he could do very little. There is
no report of any of his subordinates attempting to carry out his
promise of interceding with either Arab or British in Zanzibar.
Mirambo was once more left to depend upon his own resources
to secure his goals. He carefully abstained from interfering with
Arab caravans, and he continued to attempt opening communications with Barghash and Kirk. They answered Mirambo's letters
courteously, but their attitude remained the same.

THE DEATH OF MIRAMBO

Checked once again in his diplomatic endeavors, Mirambo continued meantime to busy himself in the details of the seasonal
campaigns required for the good health of his military state.
There are indications that he might have been wearying of the
exigencies of this life. Toward the end of 1882, following minor
hostilities which Mirambo blamed on the Arabs, Mirambo informed a missionary that "he would never go to war any more
if they [the Arabs] would let him live in peace; for he had been
fighting ever since he was a little boy; and now the only fighting
he wanted to do was fighting with elephants in the forest."[7] But
it was not a time for quiet. During 1883 and 1884 the campaigns
proved among the most difficult Mirambo had yet directed. The
Urambo *ntemi* had at last met a Nyamwezi rival who, without
Arab support, was able to fight him to a standstill. His uncle
Kapela, *ntemi* of Ukune, a state located not too far from Urambo,
was an extremely vigorous and militarily capable chieftain who
had never accepted his relative's claims to predominance. Kapela
moreover strengthened his independence by becoming an ally
of one of Mirambo's other principal Nyamwezi rivals, Isike of
Unyanyembe. And to add to the difficulties facing Mirambo, he
developed a quarrel with his heretofore loyal Ngoni allies. Following the defeat of Simba of Usawila, Mirambo determined that
the Ngoni had stolen some of the booty in cattle which should

7 Willoughby to Thomson, Nov. 27, 1882, Central Africa, 1881-82, CCWM.

have gone to him. He readied an expedition against them. The move was apparently the culmination of years of dissatisfaction. Mirambo had earlier informed Southon, "No amount of killing or punishment . . . will make them peaceable or orderly. In spite of repeated executions, they still continue to be highway robbers, audacious thieves and often murderers."[8]

Learning of Mirambo's intentions, the Ngoni prepared to dispatch ambassadors to Isike, hoping to gain the support of Unyanyembe against their powerful opponent. Mirambo was equal to this stratagem. He immediately sent ambassadors of his own to Unyanyembe; they brought gifts more valuable than those brought by the Ngoni. Although no formal settlement was concluded, Mirambo's gifts were accepted and Unyanyembe consequently remained neutral. Then, in 1882, Mirambo campaigned to punish the Ngoni, battling these formidable warriors near Lake Victoria. It was not an easy victory; to accomplish the defeat of the Ngoni, Mirambo found it necessary to obtain the support of new allies. He found them among the bellicose Masai (and perhaps also among the Baraguyu, or Humba, whom nineteenth-century observers often confused with the Masai).

The Ngoni did not accept the defeat as final. When Kapela began his challenge to Mirambo in 1883 they answered his request to join him as allies against the Urambo ruler. With their support Kapela became the most formidable Nyamwezi leader ever to stand against Mirambo. Unfortunately, little personal detail is yet known about this Nyamwezi fighting *ntemi;* he was described in 1885 by a British observer as "a fine energetic fellow with plenty of brains."[9] Kapela had few European visitors, and no oral accounts have been collected from his state. During the hostilities of 1883 neither Kapela nor Mirambo gained any signal victories. Both retired to their home states at the end of the campaign season, ready to return to the struggle during the following year.

Mirambo faced the campaign of 1884 with his usual determination, but he was not the same vigorous warrior he had been in

[8] Southon, "History, Country, and Peoples of Unyamwezi," Central Africa, 1880, CCWM.

[9] Stokes to Lang, Sept. 23, 1885, G3.A6/02, CMS.

earlier years. A disease of the throat, perhaps cancer, was troubling the Urambo *ntemi*, and unfortunately, since Southon's successors at Urambo did not include a medical missionary, there was no chance of modern treatment. Although Mirambo henceforth tried his best to drive his body to its accustomed feats of participatory leadership, willpower was not enough to restore either his health or the vigor of his leadership. Nevertheless, despite his decline in health and the threat of Kapela, Mirambo undertook a major expedition against the powerful African state of Burundi, allied with a Ha ruler seeking to regain territory earlier lost to the Rundi. When the opposing forces met in battle, at Murole mountain, Mirambo and his allies were decisively defeated.

Mirambo had little time to waste in regret for the defeat; he had to return to the interrupted war against Kapela. In this campaign Mirambo fought again alongside Masai or Baraguyu allies; Kapela with Ngoni allies and Nyamwezi supporters from Unyanyembe. Eventually Mirambo's warriors cleared those of Kapela from the field; then Kapela was besieged in his own village, a strongly fortified and well-defended center which Mirambo's forces were unable to overrun. Mirambo, because of his precarious health, left much of the direction of this campaign to his brother Mpandashalo (or Kilunga), but as hostilities dragged on without the defeat of Kapela, the Urambo leader rejoined his warriors with the hope of inspiring them to victory. Mirambo courageously walked the long distance from his home to the camp of his men before Kapela's village, despite the fact that his illness had become more severe. But once arrived at the field of battle, Mirambo's former vigor seemed to return as he directed his warriors in the attack against Kapela. During one episode of the seige Kapela called for a truce to allow discussions for a settlement of the hostilities. When Mirambo and a few followers approached the besieged center to talk as requested, a hidden group of Kapela's men opened fire. They missed Mirambo, who bravely had advanced although he feared such a stratagem, and a hidden body of Mirambo's supporters, waiting upon the order of their leader, soon cleared the field and returned Mirambo to safety.

The new inspiration Mirambo brought to his men not with-
standing, they did not succeed in capturing Kapela's resolutely
defended stronghold. The prolonged campaign began to drain
the limited reserves of strength Mirambo had used to the full in
hoping to defeat Kapela. By the end of November the Urambo
ntemi was so weakened that he had to direct operations, as best
he could, while confined to a hut located near the battlefield. He
received a few European visitors, French and British missionaries
from nearby stations, during these difficult days, and early in
December, realizing that he was in a very dangerous physical
condition, Mirambo sent to them requesting any medicines which
might restore his health. But it proved to be too late for his
European friends to bring help, and probably nothing they could
have done would have saved Mirambo. The suffering Nyamwezi
leader died from the effects of his throat malady on December 2,
1884. One local tradition records that Mirambo's warriors,
realizing that the end was near, strangled their ruler.[10] As related
earlier, this action was a customary procedure when a Nyamwezi
ntemi, the symbol of the state, was in a terminal illness. There
also survives the oft-told tale that Mirambo died from poison
administered either through agents of Isike or of the Arabs of
Unyanyembe. There is no foundation for the story: Mirambo
died from an illness known and observed by the several European
witnesses who visited him in the last few months before his death.

THE COLLAPSE OF MIRAMBO'S STATE

The death of their leader was a morale-shattering blow to the
Nyamwezi of Urambo. But the loss had to be faced and during
December 1884 and January 1885 the customary proceedings
were held to determine the selection of the next ruler of Urambo.
At one point during the dynastic deliberations, one of Mirambo's
former chief headmen asked the British missionary and caravan
leader Charles Stokes "very knowingly" which potential candidate he preferred, but Stokes quickly informed the questioner
of his neutrality in this African internal political problem.[11]

[10] Diedrich Westermann, *Geschichte Africas* (Köln, 1952), 368.
[11] Stokes to Lang, Dec. 18, 1885, G3.A6/02, CMS.

Since the Africans of the interior were justifiably not always sure
if the individual Britons they encountered were really subordinate agents of their consul in Zanzibar (John Morton, for example, while working for the Church Missionary Society, had falsely
described himself to Africans and Arabs as an accredited British
agent), the question to Stokes was probably an effort to win
British backing for a new ruler. A specific reason for the request
could have been the reported quarrel over the succession between
those Nyamwzi backing a son of Mirambo and those supporting
his brother.

In January 1885 the discussions closed and a new *ntemi* was at
last chosen. He was Mpandashalo, the warrior brother of Mirambo, who had served his deceased leader loyally, if unimaginatively,
during many campaigns. The designated *ntemi* was a well-meaning man, ready to do his utmost to carry on in the tradition of
Mirambo. Mpandashalo, however, unfortunately was no equal
successor to Mirambo, and all Unyamwezi knew it. Immediate
disheartenment spread through the ranks of the men besieging
Kapela, eventually causing the campaign to end without victory
for the Urambo army. And as the news of Mirambo's death became generally known throughout the territories formerly subject
to Urambo, the local leaders once fearfully obedient to Mirambo's
orders quickly began to act to regain their lost independence. By
February, for example, the Church Missionary Society man
Charles Wise expressed regret that many of the previously defer-
ential petty chiefs along the route to Lake Victoria were again
charging passage money to Europeans, a state of affairs Mirambo
had ended a few years earlier.[12]

Mpandashalo strove energetically to halt the mounting fissip-
arous tendencies among Mirambo's former subjects, but this
brave and genial *ntemi,* from European accounts a bit too much
addicted to drink, simply did not possess the talents necessary
to carry on his predecessor's work effectively. Even the White
Fathers, who had recently established their long-desired station
in Mirambo's dominions, recognized the imminent decline of
Urambo; they decided to evacuate their location because the

12 Wise to Lang, Feb. 27, 1885, CMS.

spreading political unrest made their work impossible. Thus, although Mpandashalo's Urambo heartland remained securely loyal, and although some outlying leaders, such as Chasama of Msalala, rendered Mpandashalo allegiance, Mirambo's unified state was suddenly no more. And other Nyamwezi leaders now came forward to contend for a paramount role in Unyamwezi, reducing Mpandashalo to being only one of a listing of competing rivals which included Kapela of Ukune, Ntinginya of Usongo, and Isike of Unyanyembe. The leaderless Arabs of Unyanyembe remained too weak and disorganized to take any advantage of the changed conditions of political life in Unyamwezi.

Kapela probably had the best chance to secure Mirambo's lost position of leadership in the initial struggles of 1885. But a serious arm wound sustained during the continuing hostilities of that year temporarily removed him from the competition at an important moment. Once recovered, however, Kapela became for a time the most vital leader among Mirambo's survivors. During 1886 Kapela, with the support of his Ngoni allies, plus the aid of many of Mirambo's former supporters, developed into such a serious threat to Mpandashalo that the Urambo *ntemi* reversed his state's standard policy of hostility to Unyanyembe to send to Isike and the Arabs asking for aid in bringing peace to Unyamwezi. The proffered alliance was refused since Isike had no intention of working for any cause but his own planned domination of Unyamwezi. Also in 1886, and again in 1888, it was reported that Mpandashalo had sought the aid of Mwanga of Buganda, the successor to Mutesa who had died in 1884, to blunt Kapela's thrust, but the Ganda leader, if his intervention was ever really sought, had problems enough of his own to occupy his energies without venturing into distant Unyamwezi.[13] By 1888 Kapela was the most powerful leader of the Nyamwezi north of Unyanyembe. He was so dominant that the Church Missionary Society men who had to traverse these territories on their way to Lake Victoria recognized the new political realities by expressing their senti-

[13] Livinhac in *Les Missions Catholiques*, 18 (1886), 610; Gordon to Lang, May 22, 1888, G3.A5/03, CMS; Euan Smith to Salisbury, Jan. 2, 1889, enclosing Ashe to Euan Smith, Dec. 1888, F.O. 84/1975, PRO.

ments that Kapela, since he could ensure their security, should be vigorously supported as the logical replacement to Mirambo. Kapela recognized their usefulness, as did all his other Nyamwezi rivals, and he moved, much to the discomfort of Mpandashalo, to enter into regular relations with Europeans. But before he had sufficient time to stabilize the growing power of his state, Kapela died, from an unspecified cause, in 1889. His state then disintegrated even more quickly than had Mirambo's in 1884 and 1885. Kapela could have been a worthy successor to Mirambo, but his period of successful activity was much too brief to allow him the opportunity of re-creating in lasting fashion Mirambo's dominance in Unyamwezi.

Mpandashalo did not long survive Kapela. He valiantly attempted to hold together his brother's declining state until June 1890 when he was badly wounded while fighting against the Ngoni invaders of a Urambo village. Mpandashalo either bled to death from his wound or, again according to a local tradition, was killed in the traditional manner by his own followers.[14] His successor Katuga, one of Mirambo's sons, was a ten- or eleven-year-old youth who, through his regents, provided little effective leadership for Urambo. He reigned until 1895 when the German rulers of Unyamwezi replaced him. But the successors to Mpandashalo made little difference to Urambo's declining fortunes. The Germans had taken control over Urambo in 1890, a move welcomed by much of the population because of the continued depredations of the Ngoni. The new European rulers gained the informal aid of the resident members of the London Missionary Society.

14 Westermann, *Geschichte Afrikas,* 368.

VIII

MIRAMBO'S PLACE IN HISTORY

MIRAMBO THE STATE BUILDER

MIRAMBO'S RIGHTFUL PLACE in the history of East Africa may perhaps be best evaluated by comparing the varied aspects of his career with the similar endeavors of other notable East African leaders of his era. The African rulers arbitrarily selected for comparison include Mutesa I of the Ganda, Kabarega of the Nyoro, Mkwawa of the Hehe, Rindi of the Chagga, Nyungu ya Mawe of the Kimbu, Isike of the Nyamwezi of Unyanyembe, and Barghash bin Said, the Arab sultan of Zanzibar. One particularly important standard of comparison involves Mirambo's efforts at creating a stable state from among the many peoples he conquered in and around Unyamwezi. Exact parallels, in this and the following comparisons, are of course impossible for the careers of the leaders of different peoples, all facing different problems, but a general estimation of the strengths and weaknesses of the Urambo ruler can emerge from this process of historical analysis.

The most powerful East African contemporary of Mirambo was Mutesa I, ruler of Buganda from 1856 to 1884, a time span almost concurrent with Mirambo's career as *ntemi* of Uyowa and Urambo. Both African rulers began and ended their careers free of the devastating restraints imposed on indigenous East African sovereigns by their European conquerors in the years after 1885. Mutesa succeeded to the rule of one of East Africa's most im-

East African coastal city-states. From 1813 Said bin Sultan strove to bring them firmly under his rule. It was a slow and difficult task, but by the final defeat in 1839 of his most stubborn coastal opponents, the Arab Mazrui family, the rulers of Mombasa, Said bin Sultan once and for all emerged as the single dominant force upon the East African coast from the Somali regions to the Portuguese holdings in Mozambique. In the course of the often violent proceedings, especially at the tenacious center of Mombasa, the Omani ruler had made several visits to East Africa, notably to the fertile island of Zanzibar. This low-lying island, possessing one of the most enjoyable tropical climates on earth, had an adequate harbor and was protected by its twenty-mile distance from the African mainland against all potentially hostile African peoples. Said bin Sultan, already as much a merchant prince as a political ruler, was impressed by the potentialities of Zanzibar for extensive commercial and agricultural development, as well as by an environment much more favorable than that provided by his harsh Arabian homeland. Consequently, in 1840 he, in effect, permanently transferred the capital of his widespread dominions to Zanzibar.

While this extremely capable Arabian ruler was consolidating his dynastic claims to the East African coast, the African populations of the interior, above all the Nyamwezi, were reaching a stage of political evolution which made permanent contact possible between their home areas and the coast. Long-distance trade, in East Africa as in other parts of the world, requires stable political entities to provide the safe routes and the secure markets necessary for conditions of profitable exchange. There are indications that such conditions were beginning to be present by the 1780's. According to Ganda traditions, the African state of Buganda, which was located to the north of Lake Victoria and which was already emerging as one of Africa's most centralized political entities, then began to receive commodities originating from the East African coast. It is possible that these foreign imports were carried, at least through part of the long distance inland, to Buganda by the Nyamwezi. The details are yet unclear, but we do know that political development along the trade routes was then sufficiently under way to allow Nyamwezi traders to begin moving successfully to the coast. They reached the coastal regions by at least 1800. With this significant breakthrough accomplished, the Nyamwezi only had to take advantage of the commercial and agricultural developments which Said bin Sultan later brought about to become the major trading people operating on the routes leading inland from the several small ports located on the coast opposite Zanzibar.

Said bin Sultan met the opportunity offered by the inland African traders, becoming therefore the real founder of modern East Africa, providing it a geographical and cultural focus and framework which still remains despite the many great changes wrought by the British and German conquerors of the nineteenth and twentieth centuries and their independent African successors. The Arab ruler pursued a series of policies destined to develop the port of Zanzibar, a center described in 1799 by a British officer as possessing only "some few houses, and the rest are huts of straw mat,"[5] as the political, maritime, and commercial hub of the East African world. It was a formidable task; even as late as 1839 an American missionary visitor said slightingly of Zanzibar: "Most of the buildings are mere huts, built of mud and sticks."[6] Said bin Sultan's success can be measured from the fact that European visitors of the later nineteenth century were impressed enough at the result of his handiwork to describe Zanzibar as "the Paris of East Africa."

Said bin Sultan's first important step was to establish Zanzibar as the one significant commercial entrepôt for his entire East African dominions. Thus, once all rivals to Said bin Sultan's predominance were quieted, and the hitherto minor port of Zanzibar became an entirely secure base, the island was ready to attract the first vital segment of the new system, merchants from India. (We will use the nineteenth-century designation of India to cover the area located within the modern states of India and Pakistan.) In limited numbers, such individuals, both Muslim and Hindu, had already become active along the East African

5 Quoted in F. B. Pearce, *Zanzibar: The Island Metropolis of Eastern Africa* (New York, 1967), 187.
6 "Extracts from the Journal of Mr. Hume," *The Missionary Herald*, 36 (1840), 60.

coast; they were virtually the only agents available to Zanzibar's ruler with the necessary skills and capital for the achievement of his aims. The Indian merchants, usually possessing ties to the wealthy mercantile houses of Bombay, the western Indian Ocean's most important commercial center, had long been active in Said bin Sultan's Arabian capital of Muscat. His enlightened policies had drawn about 2000 Indians there by 1840. With a similarly profitable existence made possible in Zanzibar and along the littoral of East Africa, the Indian merchants began to establish there in slowly increasing numbers. Providing the financial resources and commercial experience lacking among the Arabian and African subjects of Said bin Sultan, their importance, both for Zanzibar and for the Nyamwezi, cannot be overstressed, especially during and after the 1830's when one of their number always served as the Customs Master of the Zanzibar African dominions. This official held the most important position in Said bin Sultan's very limited bureaucracy. The Customs Master received his office for the payment of an annual sum to the sultan. The amount formed practically the entire revenues of the Arabian ruler, and, since the sum was insufficient for the expensive tastes of Said bin Sultan and his successors, they soon fell into debt to their Indian subordinate. In 1871, for example, Sultan Barghash bin Said owed the firm of the Customs Master $540,003. Thus, in many ways, the occupant of the office was virtually the first minister of Zanzibar. Without his willing agreement the sultan lacked the means to muster sufficient resources for any new policies. And, with the Customs Master's natural interest in the development of commerce, the latter naturally played a major role in the organizing of the Arab community resident among the Nyamwezi of the Unyanyembe chiefdom.

Said bin Sultan's second step was to develop a commercial milieu for the Indians to operate in profitably. One major advance came with his introduction of the cultivation of cloves into Zanzibar and its neighboring island, Pemba, during the years around 1820. This spice, originally brought through the efforts of Pierre Poivre from the Dutch East Indian islands to Ile de France and Bourbon in the eighteenth century, was tried out both in Zanzibar and in Pemba. Said bin Sultan was determined that all his subjects should support his experiment; local tradition says that he ordered them to plant three clove trees for every coconut palm that they owned. Conditions for growth proved ideal and both islands soon were on a path of development which made them the world's largest producers of cloves. In 1859, for example, Zanzibar exported 4,860,000 pounds of cloves. By the mid-twentieth century Zanzibar and Pemba were producing over 80 per cent of the world harvest of the crop, with an average annual production of about 11,000 tons. The success of this important experiment had significant consequences for the African mainland. Cloves are harvested twice yearly, the operation requiring a large labor force since the marketable spice is the product of the buds of the tree, which have to be picked within a relatively short period. Zanzibar's indigenous African inhabitants, whose land was progressively taken for the growth of the clove trees, were not numerous enough to handle the crop, even if they had proved willing, and therefore from this time forward a continuously increasing number of slaves from the mainland was necessary to secure a successful harvest.

Allied to the creation of a desirable export crop for Zanzibar were Said bin Sultan's next steps designed to draw other foreign traders, in addition to the Indians, to his African entrepôt. European traders had visited Zanzibar from before the first years of Said bin Sultan's reign, particularly in search of slaves, but their numbers had gradually dwindled during the early nineteenth century, notably after the Moresby Treaty of 1822, which the Arab ruler had signed with Great Britain, forbidding within his dominions the selling of slaves to the subjects of Christian nations. However, while British, French, and other Europeans were slow to rise to the opportunities offered by the new legitimate commercial center of Zanzibar, American merchants, particularly from New England, in the search for new outlets for their maritime enterprise began to investigate the commercial possibilities of the East African ports. Reaching Zanzibar, probably during the second half of the decade after 1810, the Americans found the unregulated commercial life of the island port little to their liking. They emphatically complained about the varying port charges and customs duties charged by the sultan's officials.